Can Cuba Survive?

Can Cuba Survive?

An interview with Fidel Castro

by Beatriz Pagés

Translated by Mary Todd

OCEAN

The publisher gratefully acknowledges the assistance of
Editorial José Martí and UFO Services of Havana, Cuba.

Cover design by David Spratt

ISBN paper 1 875284 58 3
ISBN cloth 1 875284 55 9

First edition, 1992

Published by Ocean Press,
GPO Box 3279GG, Melbourne, Victoria 3001, Australia
Distributed in the USA by The Talman Company,
131 Spring Street, Suite 201E-N, New York, NY 10012, USA
Distributed in Britain and Europe by Central Books,
99 Wallis Road, London E9 5LN, Britain
Distributed in Southern Africa by Grassroots Books,
PO Box A267, Avondale, Harare, Zimbabwe
Distributed in Australia by Astam Books,
162-8 Parramatta Road, Stanmore, NSW 2048, Australia

Contents

Publisher's note

In May 1991, the editor of the Mexican weekly magazine *Siempre!*, Beatriz Pagés, conducted the following interview with Cuban President Fidel Castro. The interview lasted a total of seven hours and has been edited for publication in this volume.

Fidel Castro is the president of the Cuban Council of Ministers and the Council of State as well as the first secretary of the Central Committee of the Communist Party of Cuba.

This book was originally published in a Spanish edition in Havana, Cuba as *Presente y futuro de Cuba* (The present and future of Cuba) by the Office of Publications of the Council of State. Another edition was published by Editorial Diana of Mexico.

The publishers would like to express their appreciation for the assistance provided by Félix Sautié of UFO Services of Havana, Cuba; Jorge Timossi of the Latin American Literary Agency; Maribel Ibañez; and Mary Todd.

CHAPTER 1

Eastern Europe and beyond — can socialism survive?

Beatriz Pagés: Will the Cuban socialist system survive, now that the fall of the communist regimes in Eastern Europe seems to confirm the failure of Marxism-Leninism?

Fidel Castro: I think it will. We can — and must — survive. This is a duty to our homeland and our ideas, which I don't consider to have failed.

It cannot be categorically stated that Marxism-Leninism has failed, because Marxism-Leninism has already given the world a great deal. What can be said is that it has suffered a setback — a considerable, but temporary and transitory setback. Marxism-Leninism inspired the revolutionary movement of the world for nearly 80 years. Marxism began to inspire it more than 100 years ago, and Leninism some 80 years ago. Lenin has had a great influence throughout most of this century.

Those ideas were responsible, first of all, for the October Revolution, one of the greatest events of this century, which led to the creation of the first socialist country in the history of the world.

It had an enormous influence on international events, because it triggered a fear of social revolutions throughout the capitalist world and an awakening to what had to be done — not out of generosity, kindness or philanthropy, but to prevent socialist revolutions. Capitalism took on the task of avoiding or slowing its

1

definitive collapse.

The ideas of Marxism-Leninism inspired the revolutionary movement for entire decades, and that first socialist country played the key role in defeating fascism — at a cost of over 20 million lives. That was completely apart from the errors that are part and parcel of all human activity.

Socialism performed a very great service for humanity by playing that decisive role in the defeat of fascism. Inspired by Marxist-Leninist ideas, it also performed a very great service for the labor movement in its struggle to achieve social and wage justice and for the movement promoting the liberation of the old colonies and an end to colonialism. Those ideas guided the liberation struggles in all continents, all over the world.

Marxist-Leninist ideas were very important to us; they opened our eyes to the reality of the world in which we lived. Without Marxism-Leninism, we wouldn't have had a coherent explanation of that world. We, too, as a nation and a people, are grateful for those ideas.

Beatriz Pagés: So the world can't sign socialism's death certificate yet?

Fidel Castro: There shouldn't be any tolling of bells. Nobody can say that socialism and socialists, Marxist and Leninist ideas have had their swan song. The feudal monarchical system was restored after the French Revolution — that is, the capitalist revolution. There was a huge wave of international reaction and not only the Restoration but also the Holy Alliance, which dominated the international scene for decades, yet they couldn't keep the revolution's bourgeois liberal ideas from triumphing in the end. Therefore, nobody can categorically state now that Marxism-Leninism and socialism have failed.

Among other things, we mustn't forget that 1.1 billion people have a socialist system in China, which was a country plagued with misery and famine for thousands of years. Only socialism has managed to work the miracle of freeing that country — that feeds 1.1 billion people from only 100 million hectares of land — from hunger and poverty.

The causes that gave rise to revolutions and socialism are very far from having disappeared from the world. In the end, capitalism has meant poverty, hunger, backwardness and underdevelopment for 4 billion people in the world. That is what we inherited from capitalism. Since those causes haven't disappeared, how can anyone speak of the disappearance of revolutionary and socialist ideas?

Beatriz Pagés: Your historical explanation gives the impression that we can speak of the improvement rather than the end of socialism. Is that correct?

Fidel Castro: Now, that's entirely different. What I'm talking about are the fundamental ideas of socialism, based on true equality. The French Revolution spoke of equality, fraternity and liberty, but there wasn't any fraternity, because capitalist society, which is characterized by selfishness, has not been a society of brothers. Nor has there been any equality, either. A class society divided between the exploited and exploiters, between beggars and millionaires, can't be a society of equality. Any system in which some people have everything and others have nothing cannot be an egalitarian or fair society, nor can you speak of real liberty in such circumstances. Socialist ideas, however, advocate solidarity, brotherhood, equality and justice among humans, and they will take as many different forms as there are different circumstances in different countries.

I would say that there will be as many forms of interpreting and applying socialism throughout the world as there are different historical and cultural circumstances in each country. There won't be any two socialist systems exactly alike. It would be a mistake to imagine that one socialist system has to be like another. Just as there aren't any two people exactly alike, there won't be two socialist systems that are exactly alike. But the basic ideas of socialism will inevitably triumph. The Third World countries — especially the underdeveloped ones — cannot renounce the idea of programmed development.

Thus, there will be different — very different — forms of socialism, but socialism will exist. All of the causes that gave rise to it persist and are even more serious now for a large part of humanity.

Beatriz Pagés: If the causes for socialism persist as do its ideas, who has failed? The heads of state, as individuals?

Fidel Castro: Sometimes it is individuals, communities or even entire countries that fail.

I think that the first thing that we should keep in mind about what happened in Eastern Europe is that socialism arose there as a consequence of World War II; it was born of temporary factors. Socialism was imported to those countries, it wasn't generated spontaneously. That isn't the case of the Soviet Union, where socialism did arise from within; nor is it the case of China, Vietnam, Korea or Cuba. Socialism wasn't exported to any of these countries; their own peoples created it. Nobody exported socialism to us; we established it through our own revolutionary efforts.

Those historical factors have an influence, as do the mistakes people make. The way in which people apply ideas, the unequal conditions in which those countries were developed and Eastern Europe's technological differences with the developed capitalist world were all factors with a lot of weight.

The fact that socialism had been established in the most backward, poorest countries in Europe, whose economies were based on agriculture; the fact that the Soviet Union had been destroyed two times in less than 25 years; the fact that the West, especially the United States, cornered all the gold in the world, all the wealth and all the technologies and had advanced industry that didn't lose a single screw in the war — all of those factors undoubtedly helped capitalism in its battle against socialism.

There were other factors, too. The arms race that was unleashed against the Soviet Union, the blockade, the isolation and other actions that were carried out against the socialist countries all played their part. It wasn't just a matter of individuals; you have to keep in mind what it meant for the economic might of the West to be blockading the socialist camp and forcing it into a debilitating arms race. Those circumstances had a lot of influence, to which you can add the mistakes people made.

There is talk of the "failure" of socialism. Where's the "success" of capitalism in Africa, Asia and Latin America? Where's the "success" of capitalism there, where billions of people live? I think people should talk just as much about the failure of capitalism as they do now about the failure of socialism in a small number of countries. Capitalism has failed in over 100 countries, that are in a truly hopeless situation. I don't understand why that is forgotten, while, based on the experience of what happened in Eastern Europe, people talk about the "failure" of socialism. Capitalism has ruined the world; it has contaminated the rivers, seas and atmosphere; it is destroying the ozone layer; and is disastrously changing the climate of the world.

Beatriz Pagés: You're right. Capitalism hasn't had any moral success. It has triumphed as a regime of technological and military domination. That is its power base.

Fidel Castro: Yes, it is unquestionably a dominating regime in the world economy now, as it was before all this. It was like that before any socialist countries existed. Capitalism has been around for hundreds of years and some of its aspects have been with us for thousands of years. Capitalism in the modern sense is hundreds of years old, with great experience and great strength. It isn't an easy task to change that social regime.

In ancient times, there was the slave regime. How long did it last? If you study the history of Rome or Greece, from the time of *The Iliad*, the period about which it is supposed that somebody called Homer wrote, how many centuries did that system last?

After that slave society, there was feudalism and what was called the Middle Ages. How many centuries did it last? Then came capitalism. No system was eternal. What grounds does anybody have for saying that capitalism will be eternal? Do people say that simply because a new social regime has had setbacks?

Capitalist domination hasn't disappeared. Capitalist — and later, imperialist — domination has been maintained for a long time. The first imperialist war in the modern sense of the concept — between the United States and Spain, with the intervention of the former in Cuba — took place in 1898. For nearly 100 years, imperialism has maintained great domination in the world. Colonialism disappeared, but neocolonialism arose with just as

harsh and ruthless forms of exploitation — or perhaps harsher
and more ruthless than those under which people had suffered
under colonialism. That domination has been challenged by
socialism, by a socialist movement, but it never stopped being a
dominant system. It has been dominant for a long time and that
domination still exists, more or less successfully. It isn't anything
new; it is an old reality, as the people of the Third World know
only too well.

Beatriz Pagés: You say that there aren't any new bases for stating
that capitalism will be eternal. Allow me to point out, however,
that it has the weapons required for surviving longer than socialism.

Fidel Castro: Well, capitalism has the technology for dominating a
part of the world for some time. But we can't resign ourselves to
the idea that it is going to be eternal. Nor can we support the
United States' triumphant boasting, as seen in the speeches of
certain U.S. leaders, including Bush, who are proclaiming a new
era — the U.S. era — U.S. domination and a Pax Americana that
will last a thousand years. This isn't the first time there has been
such boasting. Not long ago, at the time of the Third Reich in
Nazi Germany, people talked of ruling for thousands of years.
Those are illusions of men who, at a given time, forget the lessons
of history. No human being can be forced to renounce their
ideals, their hopes and their dreams; not even nuclear weapons
can make people do that. We ourselves have been threatened,
attacked, pressured and harassed in all sorts of ways for more
than 30 years, ever since the triumph of the Revolution, yet we
have stood firm and are independent thanks to our own efforts
and our own risks. I think that this is an example that proves
what nations and people are capable of doing.

Beatriz Pagés: How much longer will capitalism remain or survive in its present form? How long a life do you give it?
Fidel Castro: Nobody can give a serious answer to that. Nobody
can state with confidence how long the capitalist system and
imperialism are going to survive.

   In general, revolutionaries have made mistakes when calculating time. Nearly all revolutionaries in all periods have believed that they would see their ideas triumph practically overnight. The leaders of the French Revolution thought that the revolutionary transformations were going to take place very quickly, yet it took a long time for that to become a reality.

Revolutionaries — including Lenin, a brilliant revolutionary; I don't think anybody can deny that — thought that the world revolution would take place immediately after the Russian Revolution. Before Lenin, the Paris Communards thought that the socialist revolution would come immediately. Marx thought that his ideas would triumph much more quickly than they did. Hidalgo and Morelos thought that Mexico would become independent immediately. In 1810, Bolívar thought that Venezuela would become independent right away and that Latin America would be liberated and integrated. Many years of very hard struggle passed before partial independence was achieved, and its integration has yet to come. In 1868, Cubans thought that their struggles would succeed immediately. Thirty years later, they achieved only a neocolonial regime that kept us under U.S. political and economic domination for nearly 60 years, until the triumph of the Cuban Revolution. The early Christians must have thought that their doctrines would extend throughout the world in short order, but many centuries passed before those ideas became the religion of the masses in the West.

In general, revolutionaries always think that the ideas they consider fair should triumph without delay. We revolutionaries run the risk of thinking we can reduce the life span of capitalism with our imaginations. I am absolutely positive that this selfish, ruthless regime will disappear. I believe so because I have faith in humanity and its ability to struggle for justice and freedom.

New phenomena will come. I think that political science analysts will have to keep close watch on how events evolve and what contradictions arise between the big economic blocs in the coming years and perhaps in the coming decades. But one thing is certain: today's world won't stay forever, because billions of people can't go on being hungry and poverty-stricken. They would rather die than resign themselves to that.

That world must change, and it will change, but nobody can

tell you when. It will inevitably change if humanity survives the ecological disasters and the threats of war that capitalism and imperialism have created with their anarchy, their immense pillaging of natural resources, their determination to dominate, their crazy lifestyle, and their consumer societies.

Beatriz Pagés: Do you consider that the political and economic changes in Eastern Europe were historically inevitable, or could their leaders have postponed or avoided them?

Fidel Castro: I don't think they were historically inevitable. I can't believe that. I can't adopt that fatalistic position, because I don't believe a return to capitalism and the disappearance of the socialist camp were unavoidable. I think that subjective factors played a very important role.

Mistakes of all kinds were made — for example, there was a separation between the leaders and the masses. If I were to go into this more deeply, I would say there were enormous ideological weaknesses, because the masses were drawing farther and farther away from the ideals of socialism, among which human solidarity is the most important. They were forgetting the real values of socialism and placing increasing importance on material questions. They were losing the idealistic component of this process and instead more and more accentuating the materialistic aspect. At one time the harangues, speeches and documents seemed to indicate that the purpose of socialism was simply to raise the standard of living every year: a little more cloth, a little more cheese, a little more milk, a little more ham — more things of a material nature.

For me, socialism is a complete change in the way people live, the establishment of new values and a new culture — which must be based, essentially, on solidarity among humans, not selfishness and individualism.

I think that the methods and mechanisms of the capitalist system were used and abused in building socialism. Many of those mechanisms of capitalism began to be used at an historical juncture in the Soviet Union itself. I remember very clearly Che's distrust of all those methods — more than distrust: opposition. He was absolutely convinced that socialism could not be built by using the mechanisms of capitalism.

I could go on at great length about these things. At the beginning of the Revolution, we held a lot of discussions here about what economic management and planning methods we should use, what methods and mechanisms should be used in the building of socialism, which should be specific to it. I think that the use and abuse of capitalist methods led to alienation and, little by little, led the people in those countries to be just as alienated as the people are in capitalist society.

We have been very careful about this in our revolutionary process. Of course, we have also made mistakes. Sometimes we have copied some of those methods in building socialism. But we have at least paid a lot of attention to maintaining and extending the values of human solidarity, selflessness, fraternity, voluntary work and internationalist principles.

That is, we have paid special attention to the values of socialism, to instilling an internationalist spirit with regard to the rest of the world and a spirit of solidarity inside the country; this is what you now see in many of our people. Our people were trained in a different way. We even introduced the principle of combining work and study — which is both a Marxist principle and one of [José] Martí — for all children and young people.

Everyone in our country who is under 40 years old was educated by our school system and at some time worked in agriculture. As I explained, no European socialist country applied that norm and those principles; no other country applied the principles of internationalism to such a degree; no other country sent as many doctors, teachers and even fighters as Cuba sent to help other Third World countries.

Those values were forgotten in most of those countries, whose people began to adopt a consumer society mentality; they began to idealize the West, the society of cars and all those things. That poison has been transmitted to many Latin American and other Third World countries. As I have said on other occasions, if every Chinese and every Indian had a car, how long would the world's supplies of oil and metal last? That concept of human society is madness, and socialism doesn't have to be a carrier of the West's lifestyle or concepts of what life should be like.

The leaders of those countries not only used capitalist mechanisms for building the economy — incentives that were almost the same as the ones used in capitalism — but also adopted concepts of life that were similar to those of capitalism.

As a result, everybody wanted to live in a style appropriate to Paris, London or New York, ignoring the historical factors that led to the development of the industrialized capitalist countries: the centuries of colonialism, the pillaging of the rest of the world and everything else that contributed to the huge gap between the countries that are economically backward and the rich, selfish, developed countries.

Moreover, I observed a tendency in some of those socialist countries to want to have the same privileges that the developed capitalist world has in trade with the Third World — privileges of unequal terms of trade, of selling shoddy goods at high prices and buying raw materials at low ones. I noted that more than once — not among the Soviets; the Soviets never thought that way. But I did see that situation in other countries. All of those factors weakened the ideological and political process.

New values must prevail in the construction of a new society. You can't build a new society with old values; you can't build socialism with the values of capitalist society.

Among other things, those countries didn't have the repressive nature of capitalist regimes. All over the world, the capitalists defend themselves with savage, systematic repression. Only yesterday, there was a report that a million South Koreans in the streets were violently repressed by the police — armed with all of the most modern repressive equipment — and the army, with the strategic support of the 40,000 U.S. soldiers who are stationed there. If a million people took to the streets in any of the Eastern European socialist countries, the government would fall; never have so many people been mobilized there. In South Korea, however, 10,000, 100,000 or a million people are mobilized frequently, and the repressive forces repress, kill and destroy; the Western press barely mentions such things. Thousands of people may disappear, as they did in Argentina and Chile. That's how the capitalist regimes defend themselves: by making people disappear, killing them, wiping them out.

Naturally, a socialist government or party can't conceive of defending its system that way — you really have to see how the capitalist system defends itself in a large part of the world, using force and constant, systematic repression. The socialist countries are less expert than the Western countries in matters of repression. You might say that a combination of factors inexorably led several socialist countries to disaster, but you cannot say that, historically, those countries had to take that path — subjective factors played a big role in those events. Just as subjective factors are sometimes responsible for failure to make a revolution, they can also be responsible for the loss of progressive social changes. Reforms haven't taken place in those countries; what has taken place is a political and social disaster. Disaster, not reform, has destroyed socialism there.

Now, they are beginning to have millions of unemployed, all the vices of capitalist society, tremendous social inequalities and injustice — and, therefore, discontent and regret. They thought those famous reforms would overnight bring them the same lifestyle as Paris. What they have got, however, is capitalism, with all its inequalities, injustice and calamities.

I can't agree with the kind of socialism that was being built there. I already told you that we had to respect what others were doing; we couldn't be involved in a worldwide ideological war against imperialism on the one hand and against the mistakes of socialism on the other, because that isn't our mission. We have priority tasks; we have our struggles and problems. But we viewed what they were doing over there with a critical eye.

Che was the most outspoken critic in that regard. Many of his writings and reports show that he wouldn't have been surprised — just as I wasn't surprised — by the consequences. More than once, I made critical comments, though never making that the focus of my activity. Naturally, because of the U.S.-imposed blockade, we had to develop our relations with the countries that, when all is said and done, had policies that were closer to ours than those of the West. But, really, I can't conclude that what happened was historically inevitable.

Mistakes of that kind lead to disaster in a world in which the socialist countries are beset and besieged by capitalism and imperialism — with their wealth, their consumer societies and all of those advantages they have had since the end of World War II.

Beatriz Pagés: What should be done when the people ask for and demand change?

Fidel Castro: We revolutionaries demand change even when we aren't the majority. We're talking about revolution, right? Not about a system that was established over the course of centuries. We revolutionaries always begin by being a minority, and we defend our ideas and our political programs in those circumstances.

Now, I can make some reflections on this. A revolutionary defends their ideas even if they are in a minority; they should defend, not renounce them. How they should go about defending them — through political means or with force — is another matter.

I would say that a revolution that can't defend itself can't be called a revolution. That was one of Lenin's ideas; he set it forth very clearly. The first thing a revolution must do is be able to defend itself, as Cuba has shown. We exist as a revolution not because others have defended us. More than once, several of those countries had to be defended from outside. I would say that a revolution that can't defend itself isn't worthy of the name. That's the first thing about a revolution.

Of course, the ideal thing is for the revolutionaries to be the majority when defending the revolution and for them to work and struggle to always be the majority, as is true of our own revolutionary process. The Cuban Revolution has always had the support of the majority of the people. That has been a basic factor in the survival of the Revolution. If the revolutionaries are a minority — and this may happen — then the revolutionaries are faced with the dilemma of whether or not to defend the revolution. If they really are a minority, the revolution may be lost.

The idea of struggling should always be present, however. You can't surrender or renounce your principles and stop calling yourselves socialists and take another name; when you are in a critical situation, you can't stop calling yourselves communists and start calling yourselves socialists and do all those things that are equivalent to giving up your ideas. We consider that inadmissible. Thus, if the revolutionaries began as a minority struggling for their ideas, they should continue to struggle for their ideas if they once again become a minority.

The question of what methods to use for defending yourself is something else; it will depend on historical and other factors. A revolution such as ours couldn't survive if it were not supported by the quantity and quality of people required for its defense; you should think in terms not only of numbers but also of the quality of the revolutionaries. A revolution is a political battle, and such battles are won not only by the quantity but also by the quality of those participating. Even if you are a minority, you should defend the revolution. That's what I think, as a revolutionary.

Beatriz Pagés: Does that mean there aren't now any revolutionaries in Eastern Europe?

Fidel Castro: No, it doesn't. The leaders in the Eastern European countries made many mistakes, and at one point many revolutionaries were confused and demoralized. I think that many others — who suffered terribly — were neither confused nor demoralized, but were overtaken by events, crushed by what happened. There must be revolutionaries there, people who see things clearly and who were neither confused nor demoralized. But many members of the Communist parties were, that is obvious. The revolutionaries who are still there, unquestionably face extremely difficult conditions of struggle. Nobody knows how long it will be before they become strong enough to try to reverse what has happened.

Beatriz Pagés: Since the fall of socialism in those nations, some people have been saying that the world is witnessing the end of ideas and ideologies. What do you think?

Fidel Castro: I think that ideologies are stronger than ever now, because imperialism is trying harder than ever to impose its ideology and its political theories. Imperialism is trying to impose its economic ideas with maximum rigor, maximum discipline, and doesn't want to hear about anything except neoliberalism, a kind of neoliberalism taken to an extreme. There is a tremendous upsurge in the world of the reactionary ideology of capitalism and imperialism, not unlike what happened at the time of the Restoration and the Holy Alliance after the French Revolution.

There is an upsurge, an impetus, a triumphant crowing of the ideas of capitalism and imperialism, of their ideology, which is stronger than ever. How can we renounce the ideologies of the left; of the revolutionaries; of those who want to change the world; of those who want a better, fairer world? How can we renounce the revolutionary ideologies when the empire is trying harder than ever to impose its reactionary ideology?

All you have to do is read the newspapers every day; what is that triumphant crowing, if not an ideology? What is that idea they are trying to sell to the world about the swan song of socialism, if not an ideology? What is that idea to the effect that only capitalism can solve the world's problems, if not an ideology? Far from seeing an end to ideology, we are in an era of the greatest glorification, by all means and using all resources, of reactionary ideology. This is the opposite of what they say or what they mean, because, when they say ideologies are disappearing, they mean that all revolutionary ideologies, all ideologies of social change, everything that tends to lead to a world other than capitalism, is disappearing. This is a time of great prevalence of ideologies, especially those which are reactionary.

Beatriz Pagés: What are the relations between Cuba and the Soviet Union after all these changes?
Fidel Castro: Our relations have remained friendly and cordial. First of all, because we must respect what others do.

If Mexico wants to enter into a free trade agreement with the United States and take any other measure of that kind, we must respect that. Unfortunately, we don't form part of the same government, part of a multinational government, that would give us the right to express an opinion. We don't form part of the same nation. In today's world, the principle of respect for the sovereignty of other countries is sacred; respect for the rights of others is sacred — more so now than ever before. Don't forget what Juárez said, that peace was respect for the rights of others.

If the Soviets decide to make a series of reforms of any kind, including that of building capitalism, we may have opinions about what they do, but we must respect them. They have never spoken about building capitalism, renouncing socialism or any of that; they have spoken of a series of economic and political reforms, and our position was to respect their position. We even agreed with many of the things they said in the beginning. For example, they said it was necessary to oppose all income that didn't come from work — to oppose thieves, speculators, intermediaries, parasites and others of that ilk. Who could disagree with that? When they said they were going to improve socialism and socialist mechanisms and criticized historical mistakes that had been made, who could disagree with that?

The criticism of historical mistakes isn't the same thing as the destructive criticism of a country's history. We cannot be and will never be in favor of destructive or self-destructive criticism of a country's history, because as I have told you, in spite of everything that happened, in spite of the horrors that took place here in this hemisphere for 300 years after the discovery, there were also positive aspects that should be recognized. Naturally, we favor historical criticism, but not the denial of the tremendous merits of the Soviet Union, its people and its Party. Suffice it to say that more than 20 million Soviets lost their lives in the war against fascism. Three million of the 6 million members of the Communist Party of the Soviet Union died in the struggle against fascism — 3 million, half of the total. Those are impressive historical figures that cannot be ignored.

I am aware of the historical mistakes made in the revolutionary process of the Soviet Union; I have been aware of them for a long time. Mistakes were made in various spheres, on many matters: the personality cult and abuses of power — all those things happened. But all political processes and all revolutions make mistakes. If we analyze the French Revolution, we will see that it made tremendous mistakes; if we analyze the Spanish Republic, which had a just cause, we will find many mistakes. And if we begin to analyze the Mexican Revolution, we will find mistakes of all kinds, because all kinds of things happened with people shot by both sides. The revolutionary struggles in Mexico were very bloody.

We have a lot of information about this historical process. We feel proud our Revolution escaped many of those phenomena. I think that the Cuban Revolution was exceptional in that it was a true revolution that didn't have any of the extremism or violence that all other revolutions have had. Other factors may also have helped, but I don't want to go into them now except to say that one may have been the fact that the leaders were very young when it began, and the continuity of the same leadership helped to maintain the same policy. In many revolutions, the leaders disappeared rather quickly, which led to a lack of continuity in revolutionary work.

In short, I would say that many of the political and economic proposals of the Soviets seemed very good to us; we didn't have anything against them. And even when, at one point, they began to say things we didn't agree with, we had to respect them, because it was their business, not ours. Likewise, we wouldn't allow the Soviets to tell us what to do — and they never tried to do that. They had an influence, and we copied things — sometimes erroneously — but never because the Soviets ever came and told us "Do this; do that." By the same token, we can't butt into the Soviets' problems and tell them, "Do this or that; this is wrong; that's right." They must decide things for themselves.

Thus, our position is one of respect, and none of those things was any cause for conflict between us — especially since the leaders of that country have always been very friendly to us. It would be easy — and also very opportunistic — if we were to begin expressing sharp criticism of one leader or another. In general, all of them treated us well. We also had some little problems with all of them: Khruschev treated us excellently, but we had the problem of the October Missile Crisis and, at one point, sharp contradictions over what happened. Nevertheless, I respect and am grateful for what he did for us. We can't set ourselves up as judges of the Soviet leaders.

Beatriz Pagés: Then those changes haven't resulted in the Cuban government's being pressured to make any modifications?
Fidel Castro: Directly pressured?

Beatriz Pagés: Not directly. Haven't the circumstances themselves and especially international public opinion pressured Cuba to change as the Soviets did?

Fidel Castro: For 30 years, we have been accused of being a satellite of the Soviet Union, of doing what the Soviet Union did — which was slanderous, because we have never been a satellite of Moscow and have never carried out its orders. Yet now, because other people's points of view have completely changed, we are being told to do what the Soviets are doing. I have already explained why we couldn't do that and that we had already begun our process of rectification.

Tremendous pressure has been brought to bear by imperialist propaganda, with everybody saying, "Self-destruct; do what you shouldn't do." Who would benefit if we were to begin making political mistakes of all kinds, if we were to go around making reforms that had nothing to do with our history, our problems and our needs? Who would gain if we were to stop talking about socialism and begin eulogizing capitalist society, taking the orders of the United States and coinciding with all aspects of U.S. policy? We aren't about to do that.

What does the West want us to do? We are revolutionaries on our own account and at our own risk, not revolutionaries on somebody else's account, and we aren't going to be discouraged or demoralized by those campaigns. What are they demanding that we do: establish a market economy, turn capitalist? Become addicted to the West's, imperialism's and capitalism's political and economic lifestyles? Is that what they are demanding? Unquestionably, they won't get what they want. Pressures of that kind have been brought to bear, but no pressures by the Soviets.

The consequences of what has happened are something else. They have had very serious, very considerable adverse effects for us, but they haven't been intentional. The Soviet Union hasn't tried to pressure us economically. Rather, it is faced with a situation of serious economic crisis, disorganization and chaos that damages its own economy — and, therefore, even though it hasn't had any intention or purpose of adversely affecting or pressuring our country, our economic relations have been hit hard. This is in addition to the blow caused by the disappearance of the socialist camp, which also hurt us a great deal — though there has been greater damage as a result of the objective difficulties in Soviet Union. We have been very seriously hurt, though not pressured. The consequences for our country's economy, its security and the Revolution have been disastrous.

Beatriz Pagés: Since the fall of Eastern Europe, Cuba must find a new place in the world. To whom will your country turn, to China or Korea?

Fidel Castro: I think we are well placed right here where we are. We are used to having the United States as a neighbor, with its aggression, its threats and its hostility. Even if our people could pull up stakes and move somewhere else, to another part of the world, it wouldn't be any great advantage, because the armed forces of the United States are designed for global domination and have hundreds of bases and other military installations, squadrons, and fleets all over the world. Moreover, even if we could find another space, geographically speaking, we might miss our neighbor to the north. We are accustomed to it, and we wouldn't want to move, even if that were possible.

I think that we should stay right here. First of all, because everything depends primarily on us — on our ability to stand firm, to be self-sacrificing and to tackle and solve problems in very difficult conditions. Essentially, everything depends on our people, which is why we should stay here on this island, in the heart of our homeland.

Secondly, I would say that we should try to make a place for ourselves in our region, in the heart of what Martí called "our America," where we are; we should do everything we can to make a place for ourselves here. As I have told you, that is what I have always thought, and this includes the prospect of economic integration. We knew that our inclusion in the Council for Mutual Economic Assistance was a transitory thing, the result of historical circumstances, and that our definitive future lay in integration with the rest of Latin America. We don't think we are going to be wiped off the face of the earth. This island arose here as the result of some cosmic or geological phenomenon millions of years ago. Here we are and here we'll stay, for it's very difficult to change things. We Cubans have been on the scene for some time, and we are going to keep on being the way we are now or perhaps better. Cuba and the Cuban people must be taken into account.

Moreover, this means a socialist Cuba. This is an historical reality, and I think we will prove capable of defending it.

Apart from that, we should try to increase our economic relations as much as possible all over the world.

Naturally, because of the United States' policy of blockading us, we don't include it in our relations, and it constitutes a very large obstacle in our economic development. You Mexicans will understand this perfectly well. We used to have an even higher percentage of our trade than you with the United States, and all that was taken away. You can understand what a huge obstacle the U.S.-imposed blockade has been for our development. It has forced us to have more extensive economic relations with the rest of the world, struggling against pressures exerted by the United States. The U.S. not only imposes its economic blockade against us, but also pressures everybody else, with all the force it can bring to bear, to keep them from trading with us. It is doing everything it can to get everybody else to support its blockade. Some countries don't trade with us because of pressure by the United States and it sabotages many trade operations, complicating things every way it can.

Therefore, we must seek broad economic relations, and, if certain countries that once were socialist want to trade with us, we will trade with them. If the Eastern European countries that once were socialist should, at any time, be interested in trade with us, we wouldn't have any objection, because we aren't blockading anybody. There are cases in which we don't trade with certain countries because the United Nations has established sanctions against them, and we respect and abide by those sanctions.

We will try to make a place for ourselves in this complex world in which we live. It shouldn't be thought that we are heading one way, then another and then yet another. We know our future will mainly depend on our own efforts, and we will try to make a place for ourselves in this hemisphere.

CHAPTER 2

Democracy and leadership in Cuba

Beatriz Pagés: When you attended the inauguration of Brazilian President Collor de Mello, Prime Minister Felipe González of Spain suggested that you join the current of Latin American democratization. On that occasion, you replied that the socialist model was just as democratic as others. What proof is there of that democracy?

Fidel Castro: Felipe didn't invite us to join a democratic movement in Latin America. That wasn't the way it was and it wouldn't be objective to say he did, even though that impression may have been created. Both Felipe and Carlos Andrés Pérez expressed concern about Cuba because of the economic difficulties and threats of aggression with which we would be faced after the disaster in the Eastern European countries. They expressed concern and also, to some extent, suggested that we should make some concessions — I'm not quoting them — and think about how we could survive.

What Felipe said was that he knew the Cuban people were capable of struggling, standing firm and making sacrifices. He said that we shouldn't have a Sagunto or Numantia mentality — we shouldn't be determined to stand firm no matter what the cost — but should think of other possibilities. More or less, that was the gist of it. But we are determined to stand firm and defend our revolutionary cause and our country's independence, come what may. I upheld our point of view.

If we look at history, Spain herself is a good example of heroism. When Napoleon's troops invaded Spain in 1808, the

Spanish people didn't set any limits on the sacrifices they were ready to make or the price they were willing to pay to defeat the invaders, who were the elite troops of the most powerful — and it seemed invincible — army of that period. Moreover, for 700 years the Spanish didn't stop fighting against the Arab occupiers. Spain has been exemplary in that regard. In Madrid, the Spanish — including the socialists who preceded Felipe's party — stood firm for more than two years against attack by Franco's troops, who were supported by German planes and Italian soldiers. They said *No pasarán*, and they kept their word.

Today's Spain wouldn't exist if the Spanish hadn't stood so firm.

As for the other part of your question, about which regime is more democratic, I believe that the socialist system is more democratic than capitalism in all regards.

Beatriz Pagés: Why do you consider the socialist model to be as democratic or more democratic than other models?

Fidel Castro: I think it is much more democratic than the capitalist system if we don't judge it merely on the basis of what's on paper.

In our socialism — I'm basing myself on our own experience — the masses of the people take constant part in everything. If this were not the case, socialism could not exist.

You ought to know, that if the people didn't take active part in all of the Revolution's activities, we would not have been able to stand firm for more than 30 years against the blockade and threats of the United States.

Socialism can exist here, near the United States, only because of the participation of the people.

In the West, there is a tendency to attribute the merits of political processes to individuals and speak of "Castro's Cuba," or "Castro's work," when, in fact, it is the people's Cuba, the people's government and the people's work. It is customary in the West to attribute to individuals merits that no leader can have.

In the Greek age, it was thought that some leaders were divine. People said that Alexander the Great was the son of his mother, Olympia, and a god. But even if rulers were of divine origin, they cannot do what only the people can do, uphold and defend.

Who defends socialism in Cuba? The armed people, armed men and women, workers, students and farmers — millions of armed people defend the socialist system in Cuba. The first duty of a government is survival. I ask myself, in which of all those regimes formally called "democratic," are the weapons in the hands of the people? The essence of democracy is expressed in our country by the popular defense of the government. This doesn't exist in any of those class societies, where you see nothing but police constantly repressing the people.

What are the images you see of Europe — London and other capitals — and the United States nearly every day? Horses, dogs and police — wearing protective clothing that makes them look more like astronauts than humans — repressing students, striking workers and communities protesting against taxes. People are wounded and killed. All that happens very frequently.

What we see is a permanent contradiction between the government and other sectors of society.

None of those phenomena are to be seen in our country. We haven't had any of that in the more than 30 years since the triumph of the Revolution, because there is a sense of identification between the people and the government in our country. Any citizen in Cuba can say, "I am the State" — as Louis XIV is reported to have proclaimed — because they defend the government with arms in hand.

Can you conceive of such an attitude, such a sense of identification, without the democratic character of socialism, under which the exploitation and inequality of capitalism have disappeared? No, it can't be conceived of. That is why I say that, in essence, a socialist society is much more democratic than capitalism.

Capitalist society and capitalist democracy are designed to oppress and exploit human beings, whereas socialism, as a system, is designed to protect and support human beings, to help them be permanent participants in the task of creating a fairer, more humane society in which there is greater human solidarity.

Beatriz Pagés: Are you saying that democracy is a necessary consequence of socialism?

Fidel Castro: As I see it, it is both at the heart of and a consequence of socialism.

Beatriz Pagés: I understand that one of the articles of the Cuban Constitution mentions Cuba's commitment to solidarity with other socialist countries. Will that article be reformulated now that the Eastern European countries no longer define themselves as communist and have forgotten Cuba as a result of their preoccupation with domestic problems?

Fidel Castro: I think that, rather than a precept, it is a declaration of principles. It isn't an article, it is a declaration of principles and speaks of internationalism and the fraternal friendship, assistance and cooperation of the Soviet Union and other socialist countries. It also refers to the solidarity of the workers and peoples of Latin America and the world.

At the time that declaration was made, it reflected reality, but I don't think it was necessary to include that declaration in the Constitution of the Republic. It isn't a constitutional principle, but a political principle. For example, it would be more logical for it to be included in the statutes, in the Party's principles, rather than those of the government, even though you can't find fault with its content.

You know how constitutions and other documents are drawn up. Many people take part and discuss them and you may pay more attention to the content of each of the precepts than to a declaration of principles, losing sight of the possibility that it may be used as propaganda against the constitution, feeding that slanderous accusation that was made against us so often: that we were nothing but satellites of the Soviet Union.

All of those tragedies had to occur before some people could be persuaded that Cuba really had a home-grown revolutionary process and that this country has not been, is not and never will be anybody's satellite.

This isn't a pressing matter — there are many more urgent, more essential things to do right now — but perhaps when the time comes for making some modifications to the Constitution, some of those paragraphs could and should be reformulated. That won't negate the essence of our thinking: that we should express solidarity with all progressive and democratic forces, whether or not they are socialist.

Beatriz Pagés: What political reforms can be expected to be announced in the 1991 Congress of the Communist Party of Cuba? Will there be changes in the Party leadership, new leaders or new election mechanisms?
Fidel Castro: There won't be any spectacular changes, let's be clear about that. What we will do is discuss matters as revolutionaries, as Party members.

A spectacular change, for example, would be the proclamation of a market economy. There isn't even the remotest possibility that any such thing would be done in our Congress. There isn't even the remotest possibility that our Congress would approve a return to capitalism.

There won't be any such changes as abandoning the principle of a single Party — which is a part of our historical tradition, stemming not from Lenin, but from José Martí, who founded the Cuban Revolutionary Party to achieve Cuba and Puerto Rico's independence. It was proclaimed at that time that all revolutionaries should be closely united in order to achieve important historical goals, including Cuba's independence. If anybody expects spectacular changes of that kind, I think they will be disappointed.

Beatriz Pagés: What changes might take place?
Fidel Castro: Changes of political importance, such as the right of religious believers to be members of the Party. It will make our Party even more all-inclusive, overcoming certain limitations. Those limitations were brought about by the conflicts that arose in the early years between the Catholic Church and the Cuban revolutionary government. This led us to take measures that kept religious believers from joining the Party. I should point out that, in general, very good relations were maintained with the other churches.

The Catholic Church was, basically, the church of the wealthy.

The wealthy reacted by wanting to use their church to support the large landowners, capitalists and exploiters in our country. Most — not all — of the leaders of that church went along with them, which led us to establish those limitations on admission to the Party.

Since then, we have thought a great deal about this. The limitations applied not only to Catholics but to members of all religious faiths. We had taken the position that they could not be admitted to the ranks of the Party. This is an important change and I don't think it is going to be easy, because the discussions certainly were not. We have had many discussions about this, because, as a rule, our people, the members of our Party, are radical and hard to sway, and it wasn't easy to persuade many of them. However, I think that, in the end, the Congress will agree to this because it is a fair measure. There is nothing incompatible about supporting the political concept of socialism and communism and believing in God. One thing concerns what is human, and the other, what is divine; one the things of this world, and the other those of the next. Therefore, I have supported the position that people who believe in God should be allowed to join the ranks of the Party. That is a substantial change.

We will also seek improved election methods, which we are already applying at the grassroots level. We are trying to improve the mechanisms used to elect the Party leadership, but I don't think they differ from the traditional forms used in electing the leaders of political parties everywhere.

I don't know in detail how this is done in the United States, Europe and other places, but I think they have party conventions attended by delegates and the delegates elect the leaders. That principle will prevail, but we will try to make the formula as democratic as possible. The Congress will do whatever needs to be done in that field.

Beatriz Pagés: When you say that no spectacular transformations or modifications were needed, did you mean that the Party doesn't have any important problems to solve?

Fidel Castro: No, the Party has problems it must confront. For example, we must keep on struggling within the Party to create ever closer ties with the masses.

Our Party has close ties with the masses because Party members are the first to tackle difficulties and be self-sacrificing: in mobilizations to cut sugarcane and other agricultural work or to carry out internationalist missions. Members of the Party and of the Union of Young Communists (UJC) are the first volunteers in each of those circumstances.

We keep striving for the Party to set an example in all regards: an example of revolutionary spirit, authority and close ties with the masses. The Party has work methods, styles of work. Sometimes the Party interferes with the administrative sphere, but we try to avoid that. There are tendencies that may arise — a tendency toward bureaucratic work — but we ensure that the Party works with a style appropriate for a revolutionary party.

I'm just citing examples to answer your question.

Even before the Congress we began applying many measures on which there was a clear consensus. We have reduced the Party apparatus as much as possible, cutting down on the number of cadres and improving their work with the people. I repeat: as soon as a clear consensus on certain problems became evident following the Party's announcement of the Congress, we started applying measures to solve those problems, without waiting for the Congress to be held. Thus, we have already carryied out many tasks — those the Party is empowered to carry out. Naturally, some matters have to wait to be decided in the Congress. There are tasks and problems that require our close attention, action and work. Each Congress always contributes something new.

We have a united, disciplined, conscientious, revolutionary Party — that is, we don't have any political problems in our Party.

New leaders have been elected in each Congress. There are three generations of leaders in our Party now: the founders, of whom I am one; those who came after us, as a second generation; and the newest, who represent the young people who have been born since and trained by the Revolution.

We follow a systematic policy of developing and encouraging

new cadres from all sectors as well as assigning tasks to these sectors. For example, the labor movement has been greatly supported and is very strong; the women's movement, or organization, has been encouraged to promote women's interests and concerns. The farmers, the people living in each neighborhood block, and the students have also been organized. We have organized children and teenagers so that each of these sectors participate in one way or another in carrying out the tasks of the Revolution. We encourage new cadres among the workers, farmers, young people, women and different ethnic groups. We don't have any national groupings, but we do have ethnic groups.

For many years now, the Party has followed a policy of developing new cadres and it must continue to do so. Many new cadres have appeared in all the sectors in the Party, including the Party leadership. Logically, this should be one of our main priorities. Our Party is adapting to new historical conditions and new generations and is achieving ever greater participation by young people. If it didn't, what would happen? In that case, we would have a Party and a Party leadership that was never renewed, and we consider renovation to be very important.

Beatriz Pagés: What do young people demand of the Party now?
Fidel Castro: I wouldn't say that young people make demands of the Party, because they are part of the Party. In addition to which, they have their own organization, the Union of Young Communists (UJC), with many responsibilities and activities: they work with the students and young workers. The youth organization, which parallels the Party, has great powers and tasks. Young people have a very important sphere of action and they influence the whole of society, including the Party. Many of the youth organization's cadres are members of the Party and have influence within it. The Party and the UJC have very close relations; there has never been any kind of conflict between them, because the Revolution has done everything for young people — for all the rest of the people, but mainly for the youth. If any sector has been privileged in our country, it is young people.

Naturally, we also work for the others; you can't forget old people. But if you realize that this used to be a country with a high illiteracy rate, a high infant mortality rate, high unemployment, a high rate of prostitution, high poverty indexes, many beggars and homeless people, sexual and racial discrimination, you can see that our greatest efforts have benefited the youth by giving each and every child in this country a chance to study and, in line with their merits, to reach the highest academic standards and levels of participation and responsibility in our country.

Since the triumph of the Revolution we have trained tens of thousands of technicians and scientists. It is only logical that our country's need for development and for compensating the historical injustices has led us to make an exceptional effort for the younger sectors of our population — who are, moreover, the majority.

There has never been a conflict between the Party or government and young people and they have greater participation in our society than young people in any other country. Young people are part of this process — rather than a Party on the one hand and a youth organization on the other, both are part of the same system in this revolutionary process.

Beatriz Pagés: Some political analysts argue that if the Cuban government were to permit the creation of an opposition political party it would necessarily be sponsored by the United States, and this is why you won't allow other political forces to appear. Is this conjecture correct?

Fidel Castro: As I have already told you, our Party arose from our historical tradition. Even though we shouldn't be dogmatic about these matters, we can have traditions.

There were several revolutionary organizations in Cuba at the time of the triumph of the Revolution. Counterrevolutionary organizations that were at the service of the United States and wanted to destroy the Revolution appeared later on.

The overwhelming majority of the members of the revolutionary movement belonged to our July 26 Movement, but we opened our doors and always advocated the principle of unity. Why? Because the United States was promoting division. One of the most effective weapons of empires and others who subjugate other peoples, has been the principle of "divide and conquer". I think they called it "divide et impera" in the Roman era. In any case, it has always been the policy of the United States.

We used a policy of unity to oppose that policy of division, and we worked hard to unite all of the revolutionary forces in a single organization, with which we achieved what Martí had done when he organized the struggle for Cuba's independence.

It was an enormous victory for us to achieve that revolutionary unity. It has been of decisive importance in enabling us to stand firm for more than 30 years against the United States. It is the United States that has always tried to divide the people, divide forces, divide everything. Having a party was a great victory for us, achieved in the revolutionary process, in harmony with our tradition. It has been an essential tool in the defense of the country and the survival of the Revolution.

Other countries have nuclear weapons and military pacts; we didn't even belong to the Warsaw Pact, much less NATO.

Unity is one of our basic weapons for surviving as a revolutionary process faced with such a powerful and aggressive neighbor as the United States. We simply are not going to renounce that weapon, that powerful tool of unity. Introducing a multiparty system here, in the historical conditions of our country, would mean introducing division, opening the door to division — and, of course, opening the doors to division that would benefit our main enemy, which threatens us and wants to destroy us.

Therefore, I believe that the principle of unity will be maintained for a long time. How long? I can't say, just as I can't say how long imperialism is going to last. As long as imperialism exists and our country is faced with a real threat — and there will be such a threat for as long as imperialism exists, because, by definition, imperialism is aggressive, hegemonic, and seeks to dominate — I would say that we should hold fast to that principle, to that political tool, that is the unity of all the revolutionary forces in a single organization.

What you say in your question is true. It isn't the premise or the cause, but it is an element that must always be kept clearly in mind. If we were to allow ourselves to be divided, we would be making a very serious historical mistake, and we neither can nor should make that kind of mistake.

Beatriz Pagés: Many people wonder if freedom doesn't demand the right to a multiparty system, freedom of decision and especially elections.
Fidel Castro: What freedom are you specifically referring to?

Beatriz Pagés: The freedom to elect, to have several alternatives.
Fidel Castro: We have that within the Party. I was even telling you about the idea of allowing religious believers to join the Party, because what we must do is struggle to ensure that the Party represents all of the people.

The Party is the expression, first of all, of the lowest-income sectors of our population, the workers and farmers (and the workers constitute the vast majority of the people), but it must represent all sectors of society, all the people — including, for example, old people and others receiving pensions. The Party's unity isn't in contradiction with its character as an institution that represents our society. All possible alternatives should be represented in it, and we ensure that this is so. Above all, we strive to ensure that it's the merits of each citizen, not privileges, that are promoted in our Party. Our Party should be an instrument for the promotion and political development of the best citizens in the country, the ones who should have the Party's and the people's full, unlimited trust.

Here you have two things: one is the Party, and the other is the organizational system of the government; they are two different things.

As for plurality of choice, that is established in the Constitution and is set forth in greater detail in our electoral code. The Party doesn't propose the candidates running for delegate of any electoral district. Our government is based on several thousand delegates. each of whom is elected in their electoral district.

Each electoral district has more than one candidate — from

two to eight — and it isn't the Party but the people who live in each electoral district who, in meetings held in each district, propose those candidates. Thus, our Party doesn't propose the people who constitute the basis of government power; rather, it is the people who live in each electoral district who propose them — from two to eight, if they so desire. Eight aren't always proposed; sometimes only three, four or five people are proposed, because, as time goes by, certain individuals become outstanding and acquire more authority. But there is considerable turnover among those electoral district delegates. The Party doesn't intervene at all in that process of the election of delegates; it's the people who live in each district who are in charge, and no other country in the world has this system, which isn't widely enough known. Now that you have asked, I should explain how these things work.

If a candidate receives more than 50 percent of the votes, a runoff election is held between the two who received the most votes. It's the people who live in the district who decide who will represent them, and those representatives constitute the basis of government power. That's how our government works.

Our Party doesn't propose anybody; our Party intervenes as such only among its members, in line with its statutes and regulations, to ensure that the electoral norms and laws are strictly observed. We have established and ensured that the Party doesn't intervene at all in nominating the candidates. That is what we have stipulated for elections; I wonder if any other country can do better.

The fact that people don't know what we do doesn't give them the right to slander us or to adopt any kind of premise on how we have organized our government. Therefore, that right of which you spoke is implicit in our laws and in our Constitution: it's the people who propose the candidates. Neither demagogy nor money is the determining factor, as is usually the case in the rest of the world, where somebody who doesn't have a lot of money usually doesn't have any chance at all.

Election campaigns are getting more and more expensive in the rest of the world, and poor people have very little chance of being elected to anything, because they don't have the money to pay for radio and television time, publicity, rallies and planes.

In the past here in Cuba, it was the wealthy, generally speaking, who were elected to Congress: large landowners and, in exceptional cases, an outstanding intellectual or brilliant doctor who had a lot of prestige. Only rich people were in our Congress in those times, but now our representatives are workers, farmers, students and young people, who come from all over, from all kinds of backgrounds.

If you go to our National Assembly, which has around 500 deputies, you won't find any large landowners, rich people, embezzlers or millionaires. What you will find is ordinary people with merits, because in our electoral process, demagogues, thieves, embezzlers and political schemers can't possibly become members of the National Assembly. In what other country is this true?

I'm adding these arguments to the ones already given because we have a better concept and believe that our system is more developed and more democratic than others.

I could tell you more about this, but the subject may come up again in the course of your questions and I don't want to tire you with too many details right now.

Beatriz Pagés: One of the accusations, one of the most frequent criticisms made abroad against Castro is that he has remained in power without having been elected through an electoral process in which rival parties participated. Would you be ready to run for office at some time?

Fidel Castro: If our Constitution were to call for that — meaning if the world wasn't as it is, posing so many problems for our country — it wouldn't worry me at all.

I'm not being dogmatic. The governing of a country and its electoral system is determined by a series of historical factors, as I have already explained. I have always liked a good fight, I have always liked contests. When I began my public life as a student, as a student delegate, I received a lot of votes. At the time Batista pulled his March 10 [1952] coup, I was engaged in political work and was running for parliament.

It isn't that I was planning on a political career. For quite some time, I had been convinced that the revolution couldn't succeed along those lines and that we would have to make the revolution in our country as we, in fact, did. But you have to choose the right moment, wait for conditions to be ripe. At that moment, we had possibilities for political struggle, and that's what we were doing, waiting for a political and social crisis to make it necessary to seize power through a revolution. I had always thought about the revolutionary seizure of power, but I understood political methods, too, and I didn't dislike them — far from it, I liked struggle and competition.

The revolutionary process in Cuba established a certain procedure and structure. I also have to be elected — constantly. To be elected a delegate to the Party congress, I have to win an election in which many people take part. I also have to win an election to have a post in the government: first, I must be elected a deputy to the National Assembly; and then, in the National Assembly, as president of the Council of State. You shouldn't be confused about the powers of this post; this isn't a government in which the president has all the say. We have a Council of State.

Beatriz Pagés: How much power does Castro have in the Cuban government?

Fidel Castro: Any other Latin American president has more power than I have, as does the president of the United States — incomparably more power, because the president of the United States can declare war, even nuclear war, without even consulting Congress. I cannot do that, because I have two bosses: the Party and the Council of State. I can't appoint a minister; they must be approved by both the Party and the Council of State — especially the Council of State, which has the legal power to do that. I can't name an ambassador; I can't designate a comrade to be ambassador tomorrow. Presidents of other countries, including the United States, appoint ambassadors and ministers.

I do have authority, but that's something else. Authority isn't a constitutional matter per se, but depends on the prestige and respect you have; that's different. In that regard, I can say that I have more authority than other political leaders, because I have the people's support and my comrades' trust. I have authority and prestige for exercizing my functions, but they aren't constitutional prerogatives. A constitution can give you certain powers, yet, if you don't have the people's support and prestige among the people, nobody will pay any attention to you — which is what usually happens.

Beatriz Pagés: Is authority a moral force?
Fidel Castro: Yes, that's exactly what it is. It's a moral force as we understand it; when authority is based on the people's support and consensus rather than coercion, it becomes a moral force.

I can't appoint ministers, but I do have influence. Many, many times I am not the one who proposes a minister; I almost never suggest someone as a minister or propose somebody as an ambassador. As a general rule, I don't propose people for all those jobs. I have authority in the Council of Ministers, and the other members respect me and listen to my points of view, criteria and opinions, but they themselves have experience behind them and an entire life dedicated to the struggle. You don't get that authority easily, especially among Cubans, because Cubans are very rebellious and demand many merits of their leaders. Merit is the only thing they respect, and they demand that those who lead them have a meritorious history and ability.

That is why I say that authority is one thing and power is another, because I have fewer constitutional powers than any other Latin American president. You can go through the whole of Latin America and ask if any of them have the power to appoint an ambassador or minister; the Constitution gives them all the powers they want, and the president of the United States has all-embracing powers. Not even the Roman emperors had the power of the president of the United States, because the power to unleash a world war is indeed power. They say that Nero burned Rome — but who knows if he really did or if that was something Suetonius or other Roman historians invented — but Nero couldn't burn the whole world. The president of the United States can turn the world into an enormous bonfire and all by himself unleash a nuclear world war that would wipe out the human race. That is really a personality cult and constitutional — not moral — power. Those are powers that other political leaders don't have. Any other president has more power than I have. That's how our system works — I'm not making anything up.

It may be 10 years since I proposed anybody as an ambassador. People ask my opinion — though not always — when they are going to propose somebody, because procedures must be followed. The Ministry of Foreign Affairs proposes somebody as an ambassador. The people in the Ministry also ask for opinions; they have a process by means of which they make proposals, and their suggestion reaches me as a member of the Political Bureau and as president of the Council of State. In the end, I'm the one who has to sign the appointment after the person has been approved. Sometimes I participate in the process, when it concerns countries that are of special importance in our relations.

But there aren't any all-embracing, one-person powers in the government.

Beatriz Pagés: You say you don't have absolute power. Even so, I would like to ask you the following: Right now, is there anyone who has enough historical merit to replace you, or should we think that you're irreplaceable for the preservation of the Revolution?

Fidel Castro: I don't think, nor could I think, that I am irreplaceable. It would be terrible if I were to think that, and I'd be very upset if I thought any such thing. I'm not the only historical leader in the Party leadership who has prestige and influence; there are several. The others include a brother of mine who began with me at the [assault on the] Moncada military barracks [on July 26, 1953]. He has an enormous amount of knowledge, experience, historical merit, organizing ability and capacity for work. He is the second secretary of the Party.

In any case, two people aren't enough; we need three, four, five, ten. And we have them — we have lots of capable people in our country. But even though each of them may have all of those characteristics — historical merits, experience gained over a long time, respect for authority, authority and prestige of their own — not all of them will have the historical merit created in a certain political process.

You couldn't ask all Mexicans to have the historical merits of Juárez; you couldn't do that because of the role he played in exceptional circumstances in the life of the country. That doesn't mean there might not be many capable people, but none with the authority which grew out of that particular historical moment.

Let's talk about other historical figures. In Cuba, José Martí had — and still has — an enormous amount of authority; he had the merit of using his talent and brilliant thinking to unite all of those who wanted to fight for independence. They all acknowledged and accepted his leadership. Just imagine if Martí had been alive when the war of independence ended. It was difficult for anyone to equal him in terms of experience and authority. One survived — Máximo Gómez — but he wasn't Cuban; he had been born in Santo Domingo. Although the Constitution didn't deny him the right to be president, chauvinists used his nationality as a pretext to keep him from office.

Exceptional circumstances were required to give rise to such outstanding figures as Martí and Antonio Maceo. Exceptional circumstances also gave rise to the outstanding figures produced by our Revolution. Now that those historical circumstances have disappeared, you won't find people with exactly the same prerequisites. It will be more difficult to find the five, six or seven factors on which those leaders' authority and prestige was based.

I don't think this is a matter of individuals, but one of institutions.

I can be replaced by the Party, the Party leadership, the government leadership and the National Assembly. Institutional leadership is the main factor. No matter what their merits, individuals can be replaced by institutions You aren't going to repeat history so that other leaders will appear with exactly the same historical merits or the same experience as the ones who were here at a given moment.

Individual merit must be replaced with collective merit. Individual experience must be replaced with collective experience. Individual authority — that moral authority you mentioned — can be replaced only with collective moral authority; that's the secret of substitution in such circumstances.

A long time ago, I said, "Individuals die; the Party is immortal." This means that, even though individuals die, the institutions they create don't necessarily die with them. Institutions can die, too, of course. It may happen that institutions die, but it's much more likely that individuals will, because anything can happen to them, from losing their faculties to dying. Institutions aren't threatened by that kind of danger, and we have always made sure that powers and tasks are shared. We have always had collective leadership — this is a principle I have upheld ever since I began organizing the struggle against Batista. The first thing we did was create a leadership and a small executive nucleus, in which we analyzed and made decisions concerning the main problems. When we attacked the Moncada military barracks, there were comrades who could have replaced me if I had been killed in action. I didn't send those whom I thought had these possibilities on the most dangerous missions; I went on the riskiest missions myself.

We have had collective leadership ever since we began; I have always insisted on that principle and concept, because only the collective can replace the individual. That's why I say there are people with merits and ability, but it's the collective and collective leadership that have ability to spare. Moreover, if you don't have the support of the collective, you won't have the same authority; you need the support of the collective to have the authority that any one of us may now have individually. Do you see?

Now, you can't assign my tasks to any one person if they don't have the experience I have gained in so many years. One person, alone, without experience, without the authority and influence I have, can't do the job. They have to have everybody else's help in doing it. If they have that assistance, they can do everything that anyone can do individually, and much more.

Beatriz Pagés: But that other person won't be supported by a legend.
Fidel Castro: Governments can't be based on legends, nor can parties. Legends arise only in certain circumstances.

Your country, too, has many legends. You had Lázaro Cárdenas, who was legendary. I remember that when I was in

Mexico, he had tremendous prestige and authority because of his participation in the Mexican Revolution and his having nationalized the oil. He was the president who promoted agrarian reform, social justice and the country's stabilization; he had great prestige. When I arrived in Mexico, I found someone who had enormous prestige and authority. He played the role history assigned to him.

When Bolívar was alive, he had enormous, fabulous authority — the authority someone has because of their merits, talent and genius.

De Gaulle had great authority in France. There came a moment of very serious crisis because of the war in Algeria, with the danger of a coup and I don't know how many other problems, and they went to De Gaulle: "Come, please, and help us get through this situation." Who could do it? He could, because he had great prestige.

Struggles for independence or wars — certain historical circumstances — make individuals stand out in all countries. They are later replaced by others without those historical merits and knowledge, and institutions take power.

As for me, which is what you asked about, I will be replaced by institutions; that's the only way. I firmly believe this.

Beatriz Pagés: Do you consider that the constant aggression of the United States against Cuba has kept the democratization process on the island from advancing more quickly and going more deeply?

Fidel Castro: I can't accept the premise that the process could advance more quickly or go more deeply.

I think that the Revolution itself was a rapid process that democratized what used to exist in our country, and it went very deeply. I don't think that the United States is holding back anything from proceeding more quickly — rather, I would say that the United States couldn't prevent that rapid, deep-going process that was the Revolution.

The United States can influence the forms we use to carry out our democratic process; it can influence those forms — that is, unity becomes vitally important in this struggle. That unity is determined by an external factor which makes it more important than it would be if we weren't faced with those threats. If we weren't threatened, we could say, "This isn't vital. Do you want to examine other forms of organization? O.K., we can create other forms of organization." But we must base ourselves on the premise that, at this historical moment, in this situation that may last who knows how long, this weapon or that instrument cannot be renounced. That is a principle. In that sense, it does have an influence, but I don't think another process would necessarily be more democratic or deeper-going.

Other countries, that have 100 or 120 parties, are a circus. I don't think you can idealize that as a form of government or democracy; it's crazy, a manifestation of madness. Every time a two-bit leader or demagogue comes along, they set up their own party, and they have hundreds of them. Tell me: can a Third World country get organized and develop with 100 parties? Is that a wholesome formula?

Looking at Latin American history, we see that Bolívar didn't establish those guidelines. Bolívar's thinking was much like Martí's; he was very aware of the political backwardness and ignorance of our societies, the result of centuries of colonialism and many other factors that hindered development. Bolívar not only championed the unity of the Latin American nations, he advocated a high level of centralism as a prerequisite for waging the war of independence and achieving Latin America's integration and development. That was what Bolívar thought, and some institutions embodied that thinking. He drew up a constitution for Bolivia when Sucre was president of that country and he introduced a whole series of ideas within it. He was a republican first, last and always; he rejected any suggestion of a monarchy. He was very firm about that — impressively firm — and he knew what he was doing.

San Martín wanted to establish a monarchy in South America that would include Peru, Chile and Argentina. He didn't think the republican form was appropriate, because he didn't trust the reality of the hemisphere.

I'm sure that Martí, Bolívar, Juárez and others would be horrified by the spectacle that can now be seen in many of the

Latin American countries: the disorganization, division and chaos.

Bolívar was against copying European and U.S. institutions and forms of government; they responded to another mentality, other idiosyncrasies, other societies and other eras. Many of our illustrious thinkers criticized the way in which people here wanted to copy, transfer and introduce transplants of political institutions that didn't fit our realities. What have they solved? What has Latin America solved? Now, nearly 200 years after the beginning of the struggles for independence in Latin America and only 20 years before the 200th anniversary of the first proclamation of independence — Venezuela in 1811 — what is left of Bolívar's dreams of unity and integration? What do we have today? What are we, compared to the large communities of Japan, Europe and the United States? What are we Latin Americans, and what awaits us in the future?

Everyone should read history. I think that people need to study Latin America's history a little more to learn if such grafts work, if we can really achieve development by copying other people's models.

They divided us and kept us divided. They kept us balkanized as a region, split into a lot of small, weak countries. They also kept each one of our countries divided by fomenting all kinds of schisms.

There isn't even a government program that lasts for more than four or five years in any other Latin American country — not even in those where the same party remains in power. The same party stays in office, but the leader and the program have changed; each new leader feels bound to do things differently than their predecessor.

In some places, such as Mexico, that period is longer; in others, it may last four or five years. That doesn't happen even in developed, stable Europe.

They're a little more rational in Europe, because they promote the possibility of continuing a program or policy; we, however, have copied the worst experiences.

I don't know which of those Eastern European republics it was, but there was one that had a disaster rather than reform: they set up 150 or 200 parties. If that's progress, then madness should be one of the most wholesome, happiest forms of life, because all that is madness.

We have often based ourselves on premises that wouldn't have been logical or applicable under other conditions.

Now, what was the last question you asked?

Beatriz Pagés: If you considered that the United States' constant aggression against Cuba had held back the democratization process on the island? You already answered that. Now I would like to ask you if at any time — let's fantasize just a little — you were to decide to establish perestroika in Cuba, would the United States' aggression against Cuba end?

Fidel Castro: First of all, I wouldn't be able to establish perestroika in Cuba because I can't make such an important strategic decision by myself.

Secondly, if you want my personal opinion, we don't have any reason to go and copy what they did in the Soviet Union. These are two different countries, with different mentalities and idiosyncrasies. I have great respect and affection for the Soviets, but theirs is a multinational country, and ours isn't. Historical phenomena took place in that country that haven't taken place here. The phenomenon of Stalinism didn't occur here. We have never had anything of that kind, with an abuse of power and authority, personality cult, statues and all that kind of thing. There is no reason for us to rectify here in Cuba mistakes that were made in other places. Here, the collectivization of the land was never imposed on anybody; that was never done in our country. We don't have to rectify problems that don't exist.

In our country, we have done things our own way. We have also made mistakes, but there's no reason — in fact, it would be the height of stupidity — to think we should rectify historical mistakes made in the Soviet Union; our countries have different histories.

We made some mistakes by copying, but we have already learned that the less we copy, the better off we will be. I myself have never liked copying — I'm allergic to copying — but some tendencies toward copying other socialist countries did develop in our country. Those are things that happen in revolutions: that country carried out the first revolution and had more experience, and so on.

We have had to rectify things we had incorrectly copied — I'm referring to copies of an institutional nature: how to plan, how the Economic Planning and Management System works, things of that nature — but I don't think we have any reason to make reforms, changes or rectifications here that aren't in accord with our realities. Before anybody started talking about perestroika, we had begun talking about the rectification of mistakes and negative tendencies of various kinds, especially in the economic sphere, and we have been fighting those mistakes and negative tendencies on our own. This is our process, which doesn't have anything to do with another.

Naturally, if we were to do what they have done in the Soviet Union, the U.S. authorities would be delighted, because, practically speaking, the Soviets have self-destructed. If we were to self-destruct, the U.S. authorities would be happy; if we were to split into 10 factions and begin an enormous power struggle here, the U.S. authorities would feel on top of the world and would say, "Now we will be rid of the Cuban Revolution." But we aren't going to self-destruct, that should be very clear. If we were to go about making reforms of that kind, that have nothing to do with Cuba's conditions, we would be self-destructing.

History will have the last word, because many of us are suffering the consequences of what is happening now in the Soviet Union. That's perfectly obvious.

Therefore, in response to your question, I would say that, if we were to initiate a process of self-destruction and go around making reforms that don't have anything to do with our history and our mistakes, the U.S authorities would be delighted.

CHAPTER 3

Prospects for the Cuban economy

Beatriz Pagés: What are Cuba's most pressing economic needs right now?

Fidel Castro: The problem of raw materials is serious because we don't have enough convertible currency with which to buy them, due to the prices of the basic products we export, the problems stemming from the situation in the Soviet Union and the catastrophe in the Eastern European countries.

We have a shortage of important raw materials and quite a serious shortage of fuel, lubricants and other essential components for industry. Our difficulties in getting raw materials and other products that used to come from the Soviet Union through trade agreements and the fair trade that was established between our two countries — and that don't come now, or come with serious limitations — are even more serious than the shortage of fuel, which has already been reduced by around 30 percent. Those important raw materials and other products include fertilizers, metals, wood and caustic soda, affecting the production of soap, detergent and other things.

The worst problems right now are the limitations on raw materials, including certain cereals for the production of food, and energy.

The Cuban people have a good spirit of struggle and work. There is organization; there is domestic peace in our country. The workers, young people and everybody else are working hard to overcome these difficulties. However, we do have objective difficulties that create problems for us.

Beatriz Pagés: How is Cuba going to tackle the food problem, in view of this double blockade?

Fidel Castro: We export some foodstuffs and import others. The other socialist countries used to supply us with a large percentage of the foods we didn't produce here: wheat, certain other cereals, lard and powdered milk, for which we exchanged our products. We had trade agreements with fair prices for our exports — which has always been a Third World demand — and, by exporting our sugar, nickel, citrus fruits and other products (we have been creating very important new lines for export in the last few years) at fair prices, we had managed to overcome the phenomenon of unequal terms of trade in our economic relations with the other socialist countries. All that disappeared quite abruptly.

Our trade with the Soviet Union has been hit hard, and our trade with the other Eastern European socialist countries practically disappeared. We used to import a part of the cereals and other foodstuffs we needed. A large part of those imports came from the Soviet Union and other socialist countries. Our imports from the Soviet Union have been considerably held up or reduced, and those from the other Eastern European countries disappeared, due to the difficulties those countries have. They will have to be replaced with purchases in convertible currency — that we don't have. To get that money, we will have to create new exports. In addition, there are problems of transportation, because the merchant fleets of the Soviet Union and other socialist countries used to carry a large part of that merchandise. That, too, has been cut back, and our own fleet isn't large enough to handle the job.

Searching for new exports and new markets for our products and creating the necessary conditions takes time. These things occurred suddenly, when all our programs and economic plans had been based on those pillars of trade with the rest of the socialist camp. Unquestionably, that has had very negative consequences. If you don't have certain products such as fertilizers or raw materials for the production of cattle and chicken feed, for the production of milk, eggs and other products, your economy is hurt.

We were also food exporters: we export calories for 40 million people in the world in the form of sugar. We are now developing technologies for turning sugarcane into fodder and are achieving some success in using molasses and sugarcane juice for the production of meat, milk and by-products. But all this needs time, an adaptation period. You can't do it overnight.

We're developing our food program, increasing the production of rice, vegetables and fruit. We're also making a great effort to increase the production of milk, meat and other things, but we are faced with the problem of having to overcome difficulties when we have far less raw material for fodder and of having to use science and applied technology to come up with new solutions, especially that of turning sugarcane into a substitute for those raw materials. That's the main task we are working on right now.

We're making a great effort to develop biofertilizers to replace chemical fertilizers as much as possible. These are products for the biological control of plagues and plant diseases. We're making an accelerated effort in all this as a result of the unforeseen problems which we now confront.

We have given great priority to the food program. We're working on more than 30 dams, hundreds of kilometers of irrigation canals, dozens of irrigation systems and engineering projects for rice and sugarcane all at the same time, seeking higher productivity in our agriculture, basing ourselves mainly on science. This is just a general description; it would take too long to go into details.

We're also giving a big boost to biotechnology, the pharmaceutical industry and the development of state-of-the-art medical equipment.

As I already said, we are working hard to develop medicines and vaccines against plant and animal diseases. I think we are going to make important progress in these fields, which may bring the country substantial export revenue.

We're also promoting tourist programs as much as we can, as a source of income. That is, we have to get through a difficult period of adaptation to the new conditions created by what happened in Eastern Europe.

Beatriz Pagés: Is food rationing contemplated as part of this?

Fidel Castro: Rationing is one of our most important mechanisms, because it enables us to meet these difficulties without anybody having to lose their job. The shock policies used in the rest of Latin America in circumstances such as those in Cuba would immediately force millions of workers to lose their jobs — and hope. We keep them on the job; nobody loses their job here. Whenever we can we transfer somebody whose job content has been reduced for lack of materials or energy. If we can't transfer them to another job, we pay them at least 60 percent of their wage.

We see to it that nobody is left out in the cold. In our present conditions, this creates an increase in the money in circulation without inflation. We have been forced to ration almost all products. People want this when situations such as this arise, when there is more money than things to buy, and housewives feel happier knowing that their quotas of products are set aside for them at fair, unchanging prices. The other way to tackle this would be to put those products on sale for whatever price they could get, but that would be worse for people.

Whenever a product begins to run short — not because there is less of it, but because the demand has increased as a result of an excess of money in circulation — people ask for that product to be rationed.

Take yogurt, for example. More than 300,000 quarts of yogurt are consumed each day in Havana, alone — a very high figure. It used to be sold off the ration card, but when there began to be excess money in circulation and the more than 300,000 quarts of yogurt a day weren't enough to meet the demand, people said, "We would rather have it rationed so we will get 5, 6, 7 or 8 quarts a month; we would rather have it guaranteed." This eliminates long lines and ensures that, when anybody gets it, everybody does. This has happened with several products that used to be unrationed — people have asked that they be rationed so their share is ensured.

The alternative is to lift the freeze on prices. This would wreak havoc with all those who have lower incomes and would solve the problem only for those with higher incomes — the Latin American formula. Or we could fire hundreds of thousands of people in our efforts to seek financial equilibrium, but that would be terrible for those who lost their income. We must avoid laying people off, and we are doing so: we don't fire anybody or leave anybody without income.

Other measures that the International Monetary Fund, the United States and all the rest of them would be demanding would be to close thousands of schools — and we aren't closing any of them — and slash hospital budgets by half while we, far from cutting hospital budgets, are incorporating more and more doctors, as they graduate. We even protect the intermediate-level technicians and university graduates who haven't found jobs immediately; we look for jobs for them and, if necessary, give them subsidies. The rationing mechanism has created something similar to a wartime situation. This is virtually a wartime economy, because we are trying to guarantee that everybody receives essential supplies.

Beatriz Pagés: What will save Cuba — the discovery of oil or the exploitation of tourism?
Fidel Castro: We haven't thought about the discovery of oil, because that would mean pinning our hopes on luck. Here, salvation is going to depend on us.

We have tens of thousands of people working in our research centers and hundreds of thousands of university graduates, scientists and other professionals. I think that, first of all, salvation lies in science, with its contributions to solving many problems, such as those I have already mentioned.

We are already moving toward the massive use of bacteria to replace the nitrogen we have to import; we are moving toward the massive use of zeolite with manure or organic matter to replace fertilizers for various crops; we are moving toward the massive use of biological controls in the fight against vegetation plagues. Those are solutions provided by science.

We're working to develop new techniques and new varieties of vegetable that are more resistant to heat, humidity and disease. We're developing very modern biotechnological products, medicines and medical equipment, and we are the only ones who have some of them.

We're developing techniques for solving problems of transplants and nervous rehabilitation and for curing vitiligo and pigmentary retinosis. We're working to produce monoclonal antibodies, to make early diagnoses of cancer and to develop medicines for curing cancer.

We're working to combat circulatory diseases and cardiac disorders. We're working on ways to lengthen people's healthy lives and are developing state-of-the-art medicines and very effective new vaccines. Thus, we are working very hard in all fields of medicine, which is also a priority activity. Science should provide us with much more than tourism, because it is going to help solve many problems.

The food program isn't going to create a surplus for export. What it will do is eliminate the need for many imports and provide a strong food base. This is the main objective we will try to maintain during these difficult years, when we have to place limitations on many programs and other projects.

Even if we don't build any new schools in the next five years, our system of education will still get better every year, because we have a very large accumulated investment in social projects.

During the next five years, there will be few investments in social projects, but our health care system will continue to improve each year even if we don't build any new hospitals. That is why we are now concentrating almost all our investments on strategic matters: the food program, biotechnology and the pharmaceutical industry, medicine, and tourism — especially those that will solve problems.

Hundreds of thousands of people — technicians, scientists and skilled workers — are seeking solutions. Of course, you always need certain raw materials, even in the production of foodstuffs, and we must struggle to overcome those difficulties. Nevertheless, I would still say that science offers us our best hope.

Beatriz Pagés: How are you going to solve the problem of oil imports?
Fidel Castro: We are still receiving oil from the Soviet Union and

we hope the Soviets will manage to stabilize their situation. They supply us with oil and we supply them with sugar and other products. It isn't based on equal terms of trade, as it was based before, but trade is maintained.

We have signed agreements with the Soviets. They have expressed a desire to maintain those economic ties. They are mutually beneficial. We don't have any complaints in this regard; the difficulties lie in the objective problems they have, which make it hard for them to meet their commitments. The Soviet leaders and other authorities have expressed their desire to protect our country from adverse effects as much as possible; they have demonstrated good faith. The difficulties lie in the objective problems they have in keeping their part of the agreements.

Beatriz Pagés: Couldn't you import oil from other countries?
Fidel Castro: What we have done is study what we would do if we didn't receive any oil from abroad. We have been working on this possibility rather than looking for alternate resources — it isn't very easy to find other sources in view of the world situation and the fact that we would need resources for those imports. Above all, we would have to look for new markets for our products. Both the Soviets and ourselves are striving to maintain the trade between our countries, as they need our products and we need theirs. We are in full agreement on that, no matter what reforms they make and policies they adopt. We already have economic ties with the Soviet Union and its different parts.

Since it is better to be safe than sorry, we have even thought about what we would do if there was a domestic upheaval in the Soviet Union that would put an end to our supplies of oil — what we would do in those circumstances. We have already made a lot of progress. We have over 100,000 oxen and are training them to work in agriculture. We are providing the population with hundreds of thousands of bicycles. In just a few years, we will have millions of bicycles. The time will come when most of our urban transportation and services will be by bicycle. Thus, we are taking decisive measures, determined to overcome all difficulties.

I think that, rather than worrying about where to get oil — where to go and how to pay for it — it is more important for us to be prepared to meet the worst variant, which is receiving no oil imports for a period of time, depending on what little oil we produce here. That is what we have done.

Beatriz Pagés: Is it very probable that you won't have any oil imports?

Fidel Castro: I can't say. There's always a risk; everything is going to depend on how events unfold. I don't think it is very probable, but the possibility does exist if uncontrollable phenomena take place in the Soviet Union — for example, a domestic conflict in the Soviet Union that makes it impossible for us to have any trade. No oil imports means just that: no oil. If we are prepared to meet that situation, we are prepared for the worst. I think that this is what we must do: be prepared and struggle, expecting the worst.

Beatriz Pagés: Haven't Mexico and Venezuela offered oil to Cuba?

Fidel Castro: There haven't been any talks about that. There is oil on the world market, but that isn't enough. The resources you use to buy it with are also very important. We have a currency with which we pay the Soviet Union: our products, including products of biotechnology and of the medical industry. We are rapidly developing the products in that field.

If we can't get oil supplies from the Soviet Union, the fact that there is oil on the world market won't solve our problem, because we would also need the resources with which to buy it. We would have to rebuild many of our economic relations and search for other markets. That inevitably implies a long, hard process; you have to be realistic about these things.

I haven't discussed this with the Venezuelans, who are our closest oil-exporting neighbors. The whole thing will depend on whether or not they are willing to sell it to us and on our possibilities for paying for it, but this subject hasn't been discussed.

CHAPTER 4

Cuba's policy on emigration

Beatriz Pagés: Not long ago, you announced that your government would gradually lift the restrictions on Cubans being able to travel and emigrate. Why was that freedom limited for so many years and why now introduce the change?

Fidel Castro: Historically, we haven't been the ones who have limited the right of Cubans to emigrate. We have never done that. It was the United States that imposed the limitations.

At first, in order to strip our country of its doctors, technicians and other skilled personnel, it opened its doors wide. The social sectors that were adversely affected by the Revolution — the large landowners and other wealthy people, as well as technicians, teachers, doctors and other professionals — many of whom had wanted to go to the United States in search of work and higher salaries before the Revolution but hadn't been given visas, were then allowed entry. Three thousand of Cuba's 6,000 doctors went to the United States. So did many university professors in all fields; the United States lured them away as part of a deliberate policy aimed at destroying the Revolution. It also started campaigns of all kinds, spreading the infamous rumor that the Revolution was going to take children away from their mothers, and waged a dirty war against us. But we took up the challenge and said, "Anybody who wants to leave may do so."

Why do you think there are so many Cubans in the United States and other countries? Some of them went to Miami; others went to other places. Naturally, most of them went to the United States, the richest country. They didn't go to Haiti or to other poor countries; they wanted to live in countries with the highest standards of living and they went to the United States, Venezuela and (when they could) Europe.

Historically, there had already been a migration to the United States. Prior to the Revolution many Cubans had wanted to go to the United States in search of work, but the United States admitted only a trickle. Our reply to the exodus of professionals and technicians was to develop our universities. We gave a great boost to the training of engineers, doctors and other professionals. That's one of the reasons for the expansion of medicine in our country. Medicine became a battlefield, with the United States trying to take away all our doctors and with us training more doctors. The United States offered them the moon, and we offered them patriotism and sacrifices.

Now, there are nearly 40,000 doctors in our country, 13 for every one of those who left. In July [1991], we will have 43,000 doctors; we are graduating thousands of doctors each year. Now, Cuba is one of the most advanced countries in this field. It's a tremendous, impressive victory.

Thus, we took up the United States' challenge and opened our doors. We have maintained that policy for all who wish to emigrate. There have been some limitations, of course. There have always been cases of those who were of military age and had to do their military service, things such as that, but they were minimal. Except for those limitations, we authorized everybody who wanted to emigrate to do so. That has always been the Revolution's policy. They can emigrate to the United States, other Latin American countries, Europe — anywhere.

We aren't the ones who put obstacles in their path or set limitations. It's the United States that does that, even though it has a migratory agreement with us, by virtue of which it should grant 20,000 visas a year so those who qualify to travel to the United States under U.S. law may do so to be with their relatives. The United States hasn't kept its side of that migratory agreement. Instead, it has authorized ridiculously small numbers of people to enter the country.

However, when somebody leaves Cuba illegally, they are then welcomed in the United States with fanfare and applause. That's what the United States has always wanted: to stimulate illegal departures as raw material for its political propaganda against the Revolution, while refusing to grant Cubans permission to immigrate legally. The European countries don't grant visas, either. If a Cuban goes to the consulate and asks for a visa, they are usually turned down. That's how the problem arose: when people illegally forced their way into embassies, they were granted visas. In that case, we couldn't agree, because we shouldn't promote the violation of diplomatic immunity. We shouldn't stimulate actions that endanger the safety of diplomatic personnel. But we have told them that we would authorize anyone to emigrate if they were granted a visa. That's been our policy.

There were restrictions on trips from the United States to Cuba. We freely authorized departures, but only in exceptional cases, for humanitarian reasons, did we authorize for people to permanently return. We authorize several thousand people to come on visits from the United States each year, but there are limitations on immigration because we don't have the housing and other resources to handle it. Even so, we are authorizing more and more people to go to the United States and return. We began this policy with elderly people who had relatives in the United States; then we lowered the required age, and now we are authorizing tens of thousands of people each year to go to the United States and return.

You ask me why. Several factors have influenced this decision. For many years, there was a lot of sabotage, bombs on planes, espionage and other aspects of the dirty war of the United States against Cuba. We had to be very careful about people going to the United States and returning, because that was a mechanism that could be used to facilitate the CIA's activities against Cuba.

That policy was changed as the dirty war was reduced. However, there were always groups of U.S. citizens, U.S. citizens of Cuban origin or Cubans — especially young people — who came every year to take part in productive activities. Those people, who had a friendly attitude, along with religious communities and other institutions and groups in the United States that were linked to the Cuban community there, kept requesting that, in the new conditions, the largest possible number of people residing in Cuba be authorized to visit their relatives in the United States.

Thus, several factors had an influence. The experience of the first people. who were authorized to go was useful. Practice showed us that not all of the people who went and came back were involved in activities against our country; this led to a gradual increase in the number of people who were authorized to leave and return. There have been quite a number of them already. It's possible that we may continue to increase travel possibilities as long as the U.S. government doesn't try to use those people to carry out activities against the Revolution.

I can't deny that there are risks. We mustn't lose sight of the traditional lack of scruples shown by the U.S. government and the CIA. So far, we haven't detected any of that kind of activity, but we must be alert to the possibility. Only the United States can wreck this policy. If everything continues normally, it is very possible that, in the future, we will do away with the few age limitations that still remain.

I know that the U.S. authorities are now worried, and some are speaking of a "silent Mariel." They are especially concerned about young people. They don't like the idea that some of those who don't receive permanent visas may use temporary visas to get around the U.S. law. Demagogy, politicking and bad consciences always bring that kind of contradiction. We aren't the ones who are worried about travel permission. As far as we know, they are.

Beatriz Pagés: What is the state of Cuba's relations with Spain since that massive petition for political asylum in the Spanish Embassy?
Fidel Castro: It wasn't massive. I think around 15 or 20 people were involved.

That was an organized act of provocation, for the following reason: we gave them permission to leave, but the other countries didn't give them visas, didn't allow them to enter. But if they forced their way into an embassy, then the other country did grant them visas. Generally speaking, it's lumpen elements and common criminals who take part in such activities, but we can't authorize people who force their way into embassies to leave the country. If we were to do that, we would be creating an absurd mechanism, one by virtue of which those who requested permission to leave normally wouldn't get entry visas, while, through unadulterated demagogy and politicking, those who used violence to force their way into embassies would get visas. Naturally, all that kind of thing is grist for the dirty propaganda mill and for the reactionary conspiracy against Cuba.

We have said that nobody may leave the country that way, and I assure you that anyone who forces their way into an embassy will never be given permission to leave, because we can't lend ourselves to that treacherous procedure. What we say is, "Give visas to those who ask to leave through normal channels, and we will allow them to go. Authorize as many as you want; we will give them permission to leave." There will always be an exception or two; we'll apply only the restrictions that are applied anywhere else in the world. That is our position.

The international wire services give a lot of publicity to all of the violent cases, using them for political propaganda against Cuba. But we won't fall into the absurd trap of giving them permission to leave.

The man who went into the Spanish Embassy suffered from mental illness; he was crazy. He went in waving a machete and threatening everybody. He was inside for two days, terrorizing the embassy staff, who didn't have anybody there who could control him. Then the Spanish authorities jumped the gun, making statements about it, which led to new violations. There were replies to the statements, and that led to the incident — which, naturally, affected our relations. Thanks to the efforts made by both parties, we smoothed things over, and I think that our relations have remained normal since then.

CHAPTER 5

Relations with the United States

Beatriz Pagés: How can the tensions with the United States be eased without Cuba having to renounce its principles?

Fidel Castro: In the present circumstances, I think it would be very unlikely that the United States' hostility toward us will decrease. That can only happen with the passing of time, only when it sees how heroic our people are and respects our people's capacity for heroism. It will depend to a large extent on us, on our capacity to confront economic difficulties, to frustrate the hopes that the Revolution will collapse, to defend our country if the United States tries to destroy the Revolution by force. Only then will the United States be able to recognize that Cuba has firmly and courageously upheld its principles and will continue to do so. This is very unlikely at the moment, when it is possessed by an overpowering urge to engage in triumphant crowing, speaking as it does of a U.S. order that will last for 1,000 years. It's very unlikely that the United States is capable even of the minimal honor that is needed to respect — as it should respect — a country such as Cuba: a country worthy of respect and even of admiration, for how many adversaries has it found of our caliber?

What threat does Cuba pose to the United States? There isn't any socialist camp now. The United States can't claim that its security is threatened or any of the other fantastic, stupid things it has said. It's simply a problem of arrogance, hegemony and its refusal to admit that anybody opposes it, in a world in which it is accustomed to having almost everybody obey it.

Therefore, it wouldn't be realistic to think there was any possibility that the United States would be willing to ease the tensions with us, to cease its hostility without forcing Cuba to make concessions on matters of principle — which would mean renouncing the Revolution, independence and everything. What good would that do?

We know the United States very well. If you give it an inch, it will take a mile. We know the imperialist mentality, its psychology, and the history of that country. This is not only because of what it has done to us, but also because we have seen what it has done to other countries, in other circumstances. Imperialism is imperialism. Its nature isn't changed spontaneously.

Beatriz Pagés: So, any easing of tensions with the United States isn't dependent on Cuba?
Fidel Castro: It isn't dependent on Cuba. It is, unquestionably, up to the United States.

Beatriz Pagés: I believe that Reagan applied a very aggressive policy toward Latin America and especially toward Cuba. Have things changed with Bush?
Fidel Castro: No, they haven't. During the eight years of the Reagan administration and Reagan's threats, Cuba made great efforts to strengthen its defenses, its fighting capacity and its ability to militarily resist. It developed the concept of a people's war with the participation of millions of citizens, both men and women. Our country is now organized and has a much greater ability to resist and defend itself militarily than in the Reagan years. Bush has been in office for some time, and we have continued to intensively prepare ourselves. The only change is that we are stronger, more able to stand firm against threats. There is absolutely nothing that leads us to think that those threats have disappeared with the new administration.

I would even say that, with the triumphalism that prevails in the United States, the scorn with which it speaks of the sovereignty of other countries and the statements of some of its officials, that this threat is increasing. Ever since the Soviet Union began to experience serious difficulties and the United States has felt it was practically the lord and master of the world, the possibilities that it would restrain itself and act with moderation have been slimmer. The only thing that may make it stop and think is the knowledge that an attack on our country would be extremely costly for it. We believe that, and we must manage — even though it may seem impossible to many — to design, organize and create defenses that can hold firm against such a powerful country, that has such sophisticated weapons and so much state-of-the-art technological equipment. That is the only thing that can halt it.

Beatriz Pagés: What is your opinion of Bush?
Fidel Castro: Bush is a genuine, capable representative of the U.S. empire. He was trained perfectly for his role. His long years as head of the CIA and as vice-president of the United States provided him with experience and he is fulfilling his functions as head of the empire. The empire represents injustice, arrogance, hegemony, militarism, and aggression. Its functionaries and representatives express that philosophy and those ideas. I will limit myself to judging the system they represent. I don't want to make any personal comments.

Beatriz Pagés: Do you think that the victory of the United States over Iraq will lead it to launch a military attack on Cuba?
Fidel Castro: The Iraqi war was a tragedy. Nobody knows how much that adventure cost the economy or the ecological effects it will have. Certainly, its political effects for the world are very negative.

I knew this would be so; I knew everything that was going to happen. The Iraqi war wasn't responsible for the present hegemony of the United States. Instead, what is really responsible for the hegemony of the United States are the problems that the socialist camp and the Soviet Union — that have practically removed it from the world political scene as a force counterbalancing the United States' warlike plans, although I don't think they have permanently eliminated it. The Soviet Union is still a great power, a great country and a considerable force, but its current problems, with its internal crisis, have reduced to a minimum its participation in and influence on international events.

The United States made the most of that historical situation, which gave it hegemony in the world even before the Iraqi war. That war simply put the final stamp on its being a unilateral, hegemonic power in the world. The United States made very good use of Iraq's mistakes.

We have to start from the fact — I'm not just saying this now, I said it quite some time ago — that the occupation of Kuwait was a colossal political mistake and a flagrant violation of international law. You have to start from generally accepted norms. It was a country with which Iraq had diplomatic relations and to which it had given official recognition. I think that the occupation was an enormous mistake and an unacceptable action.

We didn't hesitate at all in denouncing the occupation and then the annexation of Kuwait — which was yet another mistake — and then the taking of hostages, in the Security Council of the United Nations. We have always been opposed to the policy to taking hostages. We denounced all of those things in the Security Council.

However, we didn't support the economic blockade — I am referring to the blockade of food and medicine — because the blockade turned millions of Iraqi women, children and old people into hostages by depriving them of the possibility of receiving food. We considered that inhumane, and the Security Council of the United Nations should never have accepted that formula.

What's worse, the United States imposed its unilateral military blockade before it was approved in the United Nations. After unilaterally imposing the blockade, it presented a proposal and the blockade was approved. We didn't agree to it and much less to the idea of a programmed war. That war, declared with 45 days warning, was an amazing, extremely dangerous thing. Everyone knew what consequences it could have, but the United Nations agreed to the war. The world institution that was created precisely to struggle for peace authorized that war.

Naturally, we categorically opposed it. We believed that the problem could and should be solved politically. We based ourselves on the principle that Iraq couldn't hold out against the conditions of isolation and the political pressures that could be exerted without starving women and children. In the end, its position would become untenable. Carter himself said that one day of war cost more than a year of waiting. But the amazing thing was that the United Nations went along with the war.

If Iraq had been a country with nuclear weapons, would it have declared a nuclear war? If instead of Iraq, it had been France, England, the Soviet Union, China or some other nuclear country, would the United Nations have declared a nuclear war? Would the United Nations have agreed to the extermination of humanity? What meaning would that have? What is moral or ethical about a war supported by the United Nations when it authorized the U.S. empire to wage that war?

All that was the result of mistakes that the United States took advantage of. As soon as Iraq invaded, the other Arabs wanted to find a solution. The United States sabotaged all possibilities, brought enormous pressure to bear on a number of Arab countries so they wouldn't seek a political solution. The United States decided to immediately send in troops and worked the situation that had been created for all it was worth.

The United States didn't want a political solution. The United States wanted a military solution with all of the enormous advantages it had achieved: international political advantages, Iraq's isolation, the denunciation of Iraq for what it had done, a great coalition that included Arabs and Muslims, a great coalition of the United States and the other NATO forces. It got together a colossal military and political force — not only of its own, but also from other countries.

We knew how things would turn out, and we moved quickly. We presented all of these points of view to the leaders of various countries, including those of Iraq; we expressed these views to them clearly and frankly. We urged them to rectify the mistakes they had made, pointing out that they would be isolated politically; that what they had done had led to the formation of powerful military and political forces against them; and that what they were doing would have very negative consequences for their country, the other Third World countries, and the entire world. We urged them to rectify their mistakes and express their willingness to withdraw from Kuwait and to abide by the United

Nations' resolution on that country's sovereignty.

The documents are there, showing that we clearly, categorically and in a reasoned way said that they should rectify their mistakes. We even told them, "It takes more courage to rectify mistakes than to continue along that path." We described all the consequences, that they would be subjected to a sophisticated, technical war with a minimum loss of U.S. lives. We explained it all to them.

Unfortunately, our arguments and efforts, along with those of others, failed to get Iraq to correct its mistakes. As a result, the United States took advantage of that situation in order to show its power, to lay claim to being the lord and master of the world and to terrorize the world. It was a kind of Hiroshima and Nagasaki directed at the Third World countries: "See how powerful I am." It turned Iraq into a testing ground for the sophisticated weapons of the United States. It killed who knows how many people; neither side has released any figures. The only thing we now have is a testimonial to its power and hegemony. As soon as the problems arose in the Soviet Union and the rest of the socialist camp, that situation was predetermined.

Beatriz Pagés: I'll change the question. Could the changes that have taken place in the Soviet Union and the rest of the socialist world lead the United States to attack Cuba militarily? Does that possibility exist?
Fidel Castro: Even without such a situation, the United States attacked Vietnam and intervened in Grenada, one of the smallest countries in the world. It invaded and is still occupying Panama. What guarantee can the United States give any country? What security can the United States give us?

We won't make the mistake of trusting a morality that the U.S. doesn't have, to a moderation it doesn't have. We must only trust our ability to stand firm against any military aggression.

Even without such a situation, it has intervened many times. Logically, this may encourage it to set forth on yet another military adventure.

Beatriz Pagés: You say, however, that Cuba isn't Iraq and that it might become another Vietnam.

Fidel Castro: Or something worse than Vietnam. Who knows? The United States didn't manage to invade and occupy Vietnam; its troops didn't engage in hand-to-hand combat in North Vietnam. They fought against the revolutionaries in the South, who were powerful adversaries, but they didn't fight against an entire organized people that was prepared for struggle.

It will never be able to force us to surrender with a war of attrition. Its troops would have to end up fighting against us on our own land, and while the consequences would unquestionably be very serious for us, the consequences for them could be worse than in Vietnam. That is the cost for them of that kind of war. I'm sure they would have to withdraw; they wouldn't have any alternative. Of course, we don't want to have to prove this; we don't want this to happen. But one of the ways of preventing it is for it to be too costly for them to initiate any aggression against Cuba.

You said that Cuba wasn't Iraq. Of course, there are differences, but not between our peoples. I don't think any nation of people is different from any other. I don't think one people is braver than another. One people may be better prepared than another for meeting a certain test; one people may have more incentives than another.

Unquestionably, a war stemming from the invasion and annexation of another country, as happened in the Gulf, can't be a strong, convincing, persuasive incentive for a people to fight to the death. In wars, as in everything else, you need a strong incentive and very strong morale. A war that you provoke in such a way, isn't at all the same as a war in which you are defending your sovereignty, your country, your land, your revolution, your ideas and your values. A war of this sort, which has been imposed on you, is entirely different.

In such circumstances, a country is capable of doing things that others can't do in other circumstances. Those would be the circumstances in which we would be fighting. Moreover, we are prepared and have a philosophy, a military doctrine, for meeting a U.S. attack. We have been working on this for a long time. You can't do it in two months or two years; it takes many years to prepare this.

We have been working on such a concepts ever since Reagan began his threats. Laser bombs, the so-called intelligent bombs, Cruise missiles, battleships and F-15 and F-16 bombers — we know all about them: how many the United States has, how many bombs it can drop and where it can drop them. We've known all that for some time. They are nothing new for us and we aren't going to be frightened by them. To the contrary, they strengthen our spirit and determination to struggle.

I can tell you three things about what happened in Iraq: first, wars shouldn't be provoked; second, when wars do break out, you should conduct them properly; and third, when patriotic wars begin, they can end only with victory or death.

Beatriz Pagés: Why is the United States so concerned about Cuban democracy while paying no attention to other countries where injustice, human rights violations and the despotism of their rulers have plunged their peoples into backwardness and poverty? Why is Cuba an obsession with the United States?
Fidel Castro: That's exactly what we are: an obsession.

The United States could begin by being concerned about its own democracy — first of all, because less than 50 percent of the eligible voters go to the polls in the United States, and they elect the president with 25 percent of the possible votes.

Over 95 percent of the eligible voters have taken part in our elections, which are held every two and a half years. Meanwhile, in the United States the president and congressmen are elected with 25 percent of the possible votes, or even less.

More than half of the U.S. voters can't be bothered to vote, they would rather go for a drive, to the movies or to a restaurant or throw a party. They really should do something about that. An insignificant minority elects the president, who has all the resources and all the means of power for achieving their political aims.

The United States has terrible problems. They talk about human rights, but white Anglo-Saxons are never sent to the gas chamber or the electric chair; the electric chair, the death penalty — all those things — are for blacks, Chicanos, Latinos and all the others who don't belong to the "superior" race.

The lowest infant mortality rates are for the "superior" race — whites — and others who have money. The highest infant mortality rates and the worst jobs are for the blacks and those of Hispanic ancestry. It's the Haitians, Mexicans and other Latin Americans who have to pick the tomatoes and other vegetables because the people born in the United States don't do that. Other people have to do the hardest work.

The United States has problems of all kinds, such as drugs, gambling, prostitution and begging. But if you're rich and one of the most powerful, of course, you do have possibilities.

I think it should begin by becoming concerned about human rights at home. Quite frequently, I see photographs of police and dogs repressing blacks, students and workers. I see those photos and I can only observe that the United States should start by being concerned about its own democracy and its own problems with human rights.

Historically, it has been the ally of the most repressive governments in the world: Pinochet's and the other military dictatorships in South and Central America — all the repressive governments. It has been the ally of the worst governments in the world — precisely because those governments docilely went along with its policies and defended its interests. It was the ally of South Africa and of Franco for many years. It entered into military alliances with those who wound and kill dozens of Palestinians every day. It is a firm ally of South Korea, where it has 40,000 soldiers and where there is terrible repression of the workers and students every day. During the last five days, four young people set themselves on fire, burned themselves alive, in protest against what's going on there. But the United States couldn't care less. The United States has never had an ethical policy; what it has always had is interests — nothing but interests.

Beatriz Pagés: You point out that the United States has always been the ally of repressive governments. However, it is the United States which accuses the Cuban government of being repressive, of having instilled fear in the island and of not providing a decent life to its citizens.

Fidel Castro: Has anybody done more for children than Cuba? How many hundreds of thousands of children have we saved by reducing the infant mortality rate from 60 to 10.7 for every 1,000 live births? How many hundreds of thousands of lives have we saved with our health programs? To how many people have we restored good health, and how many people's lives have we lengthened? How many benefits have we given all the children in our country by providing each and every one of them with an education and giving them jobs when they graduate? How many women have we saved from prostitution? How many people have we saved from drugs, unemployment and begging? There isn't even one homeless child in Cuba — not one! But, in the rest of Latin America, there are 30 million homeless children, and there are millions of homeless in the United States, too, even though it is so large and fabulously rich.

But the United States slanders Cuba, a country where nobody has been murdered for political reasons, nobody has disappeared and physical violence has not been used since the triumph of the Revolution, continuing a tradition begun during the war. Does anybody believe that our people would go along with that or would support the Revolution if it weren't for its extremely humane nature, its spirit of justice and its respect for the law?

How many children unnecessarily die every year in Latin America? According to FAO and UNICEF, 800,000 children die in Latin America each year — 800,000 children who could otherwise be saved. Not one of them dies here in Cuba. FAO and UNICEF have said that, if those 800,000 children had access to the same level of health care as Cuba offers, they wouldn't die. Therefore, what is the crime for which Cuba should be punished, and why does anybody feel the need to slander Cuba?

Thirty million children in other Latin American countries are homeless; every children in Cuba has a home. The other Latin American countries have tens of millions of beggars; Cuba has none. In other Latin American countries, you see children cleaning car windshields, running among the cars to do that, and doing a million and one other things to eke out an existence. Isn't that situation a flagrant violation of human rights?

How can the United States speak of human rights when it has

imposed poverty, underdevelopment and misery on our countries, exploiting and pillaging them? It doesn't have any moral right to criticize Cuba. What can it honestly say?

The U.S. authorities are cynical and obsessive and don't forgive us for having been able to stand firm. That's the only explanation.

Beatriz Pagés: They don't forgive Cuba for being a symbol?
Fidel Castro: Yes, I think Cuba is a symbol. I don't have any doubt about that. I am also convinced it sets an example.

Beatriz Pagés: What are you going to do to end that campaign that accuses Cuba of being the country in which human rights are most violated?
Fidel Castro: What can we do? Can we do any more for the people than we are already doing? We have been fighting this battle for a long time. It isn't easy to struggle against the enormous publicity and propaganda apparatus of the United States. It has fabulous means by which it sends television programs all over the world; it has invested hundreds of millions of dollars in them. It isn't easy for a small country to counteract that. We are doing our duty, and our conscience is clear. History will show who was right. What can we do? We have nothing to rectify, because we haven't made any of those mistakes. Simply, we have a sense of ethics; we have principles. I think that the only thing we can do is what we have been doing: the most we can for our people, even in the most difficult conditions.

CHAPTER 6
The future of Latin America

Beatriz Pagés: What steps does Cuba intend to take in the near future to promote Latin American integration?

Fidel Castro: As I told a group of guests who were visiting here recently, our country is ready to become integrated with the rest of Latin America. If it is a matter of doing away with tariff barriers, that's no problem. If we have to do away with borders, that's no problem, either, even though our borders are maritime. I think that Cuba is the country most ready to do this, from both the economic and political point of view. There are no tariffs to speak of here; we have no kinds of tariff barriers to hinder the development of extensive trade with the rest of Latin America. From the political point of view, our people are ready for integration because there's no chauvinism in Cuba. Ours is a patriotic country, nationalist in the best sense of the term, without chauvinism and without any feelings of hostility toward any other people. Thus, in both regards, we are more ready than any other country to become integrated with the rest of Latin America. Moreover, Cuba is a country with absolute independence, that doesn't take orders or bow to pressures from anyone.

For many years, all of the other Latin American countries except Mexico broke off diplomatic relations and imposed a blockade, so we were forced to develop our economic relations with the Council for Mutual Economic Assistance, with the other socialist countries. But even at that time, many years ago, we said that our natural area, our natural sphere for future integration, was Latin America. We said that we were joining the European socialist countries in a transitional stage of our development, but that our final aim would be to become an integral part of Latin America. That has been our thinking throughout these years.

Latin American integration isn't dependent on us. We can't do much, because we aren't a financial power, a developed country or a country with large resources. Moreover, Cuba has had to engage in a hard-fought struggle against the United States, a neighbor that has a lot of influence in the rest of Latin America and that has tried to limit our ties with other Latin American countries and to sever them if possible. It has tried to divide us and has engaged in intrigue. Not a great deal is dependent on us, but we are ready and willing to do what we can. We believe that Latin America won't have any future if it doesn't become integrated.

Beatriz Pagés: Is the rest of Latin America willing to be integrated with Cuba?

Fidel Castro: The signs I have observed in recent years are positive. We have even voted the same way on many issues in the United Nations and other international agencies. There have been many expressions of cooperation and respect between the largest Latin American countries and Cuba. The isolation and blockade — when nearly everybody, obeying the orders of the United States, broke off relations with Cuba -- are things of the past. The Latin American countries now have a greater sense of political dignity, a greater sense of their own interests and a greater sense of national sovereignty.

Paradoxically, now, when they have less economic independence, is when they have become much more constructive and politically positive toward Cuba.

Beatriz Pagés: Are those relations closer?

Fidel Castro: Yes, our relations with most of the Latin American countries — logically, there are always some exceptions — are unquestionably closer. We don't have relations with some of the Central American countries. Sometimes, when there aren't official relations, as in the case of Colombia, there is communication and we have cooperated on issues in the United Nations. There is a climate of respect between those governments and the government of Cuba and I think that our relations are definitely closer.

Many people from other Latin American countries come here. Every so often we hold a congress here, and 1,000, 1,200 or 1,500 professors come from other Latin American countries, including some very outstanding figures. Every year I see and greet thousands of people from other Latin American countries and we have very friendly, sometimes fraternal relations with all of those outstanding figures from the most varied social classes — from all social classes. I have many contacts with scientists and people from many other spheres of endeavor in other parts of Latin America and they have a very positive attitude toward Cuba. The more they know about Cuba, the more they trust Cuba. Right now, in these hard times, they have expressed the hope that Cuba will manage to survive.

Beatriz Pagés: They have expressed solidarity with Cuba?
Fidel Castro: They can't do much, but they have expressed feelings of great solidarity with Cuba. That feeling is growing. Perhaps it is because we have become a sort of rara avis in the world, which awakens greater interest among Latin Americans. However, I don't think it is only that: they view the work of the Cuban Revolution with ever greater respect and appreciation. Just imagine what the teachers, doctors and scientists think when they meet here and see all that Cuba has done in their field. They feel stimulated and encouraged.

Beatriz Pagés: On several occasions, you have said that Latin America and the other Third World countries should unite to tackle the economic crisis and the debt. However, with the so-called economic globalization that is taking place in the world, the most powerful countries are threatening to swallow up the weakest. What can be done about this?
Fidel Castro: What you say is so. I made many of those statements in 1985 — quite a few years have passed since then — on the crisis and the foreign debt. Many Latin Americans attended the meetings held here on this subject and the ideas we set forth.

We said things that have proved to be absolutely correct: that the foreign debt was unpayable and uncollectable; that we should seek the unity of all the Third World countries for this battle of the foreign debt, because all were in the same situation; and that we should struggle not only to have the debt cancelled but also to establish the New International Economic Order. The call for the establishment of a New International Economic Order was approved as a result of a battle that the Third World countries waged in the United Nations. That was 10 years earlier — some 15 years ago now — and the International Economic Order hasn't been applied at all.

We said that we had to struggle against the financial manipulations, the high bank interest rates, the unequal terms of trade, the protectionism and the thousand and one other means the developed capitalist countries used to pillage the Third World countries, especially in Latin America.

We said that we should unite on the problem of the debt in order to wage that battle. The Latin American countries didn't prove capable of uniting on such a vital problem, and they lost a great historic opportunity. The United States preferred to discuss the matter with each of them individually, imposing its conditions and giving them different treatment, depending on its economic and political interests in each case. The Latin American countries and leaders weren't capable of presenting a common front for waging that battle.

That would have been of tremendous help in the process of Latin American integration and would have helped to ward off Latin America being swallowed up by the United States.

We urged that this great struggle be waged. Instead, we saw vacillation, division and the individual criteria of the leaders of each country win out over an awareness of the great historic opportunity we had at that time.

But what can you do? The situation continued to become more acute: the debt is still with us, unpayable and uncollectable but demanding an enormous economic sacrifice, with interest payments bleeding the economy every year. Unequal terms of trade are still in effect and becoming ever more unequal. We keep having to pay more and more for the things we buy while getting less and less for what we sell. The flight of capital continues and Latin America's creditors take out around $30 billion every year in net capital.

One day, we made some calculations. I had already stated at the Latin America Memorial in Sao Paulo, in a ceremony paying tribute to Villas Boas, a great anthropologist who was returning from the jungle where he had worked for 30 years, that many Villas Boases were needed, because we, the new Indians, needed such champions. We were the new Indians, because the conquerors wanted to discover and conquer us again and were pillaging our countries more than ever before.

At that time, I suggested that we analyze how much gold and silver Spain had taken from Latin America in the course of 300 years and how much gold and silver was now being taken from our countries every year. I said they might be taking out more in a single year now than the Spaniards took out in 300 years, and my prediction was correct. When the studies were made, it became clear that the Spaniards had taken out around 800 tons of gold and around 12,000 or 14,000 tons of silver, and that sums equal to around 3,000 tons of gold were now being taken out of Latin America every year.

The developed capitalist countries take the equivalent of 3,000 tons of gold from Latin America every year. That's based on turning the convertible currency that is taken out of Latin America, without inflation, into gold. Look how much exploitation there is; it is because there are more of us Indians now, and they get more out of us. There are now around 400 million of us Indians — many more than the number Spain had mining gold or panning for it in the rivers. It is an impressive figure. These are realities. As I said in 1985, we should unite, but we haven't made much progress.

We are now threatened with Latin America's economy being swallowed up by that of the United States. This is a very real danger.

Beatriz Pagés: What has impeded Latin American unity?
Fidel Castro: In the past century, it was the British — and, in part, the United States. In this century the United States has done

everything possible to keep us balkanized and divided, and we ourselves have contributed to this with our incompetence, limitations, lack of historical vision and collective irresponsibility.

Beatriz Pagés: For lack of nationalist conviction?
Fidel Castro: I wouldn't say lack of nationalist conviction. This is a long history. Bolívar wanted Latin American unity, but couldn't achieve it. It would have been extremely difficult for him to achieve it in an era when it might take two months for a letter to go from Caracas to Bogotá, or three months for a letter to go from Caracas to Lima and another three months to get a reply.

The more I read about and study that history, the more I admire Bolívar, his greatness and his tremendous vision. I'm sorry that Latin Americans aren't more familiar with that history and don't know more about him. Everything he tried to do was frustrated, because what he wanted at that time could not be realized.

It's shameful that now, when we can talk by telephone from northern Mexico to Patagonia in a matter of seconds — now, when there are planes, communications, ships, satellites and all kinds of the most sophisticated means of communication – we remain as divided as we are, in a region in which we even speak the same language. When I meet with other Latin Americans I am impressed, because although they come from around 20 different countries I can speak with all of them in the same language without needing a translator.

The Europeans, who warred among themselves for centuries and who have very different nations, languages, cultures and religions, are uniting. Yet we Latin Americans, who have the same culture, language and history are unable or don't have enough determination to do the same. This is a blot on our history.

I think that students of history, political science and economics should analyze these problems. They should delve deeply into all this and see what relationship there is between the Latin American systems of government, political and economic systems and our lack of unity. I think that this should really be studied in depth. It is a calamity and a disgrace that will guarantee a grim future.

What prospects will we have in the world of the future, which will be governed by the large communities such as Japan and other parts of Southeast Asia, the United States, Europe, China and the new blocs that are being created? What prospects do the Latin American countries have? We should become aware of this. Perhaps people will.

Not long ago, four South American countries — Argentina, Brazil, Paraguay and Uruguay — entered into an agreement and even spoke of eliminating tariff barriers by 1995. I think it's a positive effort. What with all the changes that have taken place in the world, some people are clearly worried about what's going on.

There are some developments, but a real awareness is still lacking. Everybody talks about unity, but there isn't any real awareness of the need for integration in Latin America. Everybody understands it very superficially in theory, but administrations come and administrations go; some of them make an effort in one direction, and others in another. There's no continuity of policy, which explains why this process of integration is advancing so slowly — a process that the most alert people consider to be vital, a matter of our peoples' survival.

Beatriz Pagés: U.S. President George Bush has proposed a free trade agreement to include Mexico, the United States and Canada, plus something that he calls the Initiative for the Americas, to bolster the Latin American economies. In view of Latin America's poverty and indebtedness, do you consider those trade projects to be the only way out for our countries? What would Latin America gain or lose if it became integrated with the U.S. economy?

Fidel Castro: I think it would lose the little political independence it has left. The United States already acts as the virtual lord and master of this hemisphere. That is a basic concern. I think that we would become suppliers of cheap raw materials and cheap labor, attracting industries with low capital investments per worker as well as polluting industries. We would become prisoners of U.S. technology and of the industrial development of the United

States. All this, of course, requires study and analysis, starting from these things that are evident — a study and analysis that, of course, hasn't been undertaken.

What would Latin America become in the end — a kind of Puerto Rico? Is that Latin America's political and economic ideal? Around 60 percent of Puerto Ricans are on welfare. What is Latin America going to become: one great big consumer society empire of gambling, prostitution, drugs and other vices?

As I said, the United States has interests, not sentiments, and Bush's accelerated promotion of those initiatives began very suddenly, especially since the phenomena that took place in Eastern Europe and the change in the balance of economic forces in the world.

Europe is becoming a huge economic power and the absorption of some of the former Eastern European countries may make it even more powerful as an economic entity. Those economic powers include Germany, whose borders are expanding and whose population and wealth are growing.

Japan's economic and financial clout, its production capacity and its ability to compete are well known.

Beatriz Pagés: Should we say, then, that the trade agreements proposed by the U.S. government are an effort to compete with Europe and Japan, both of which have grown stronger, and also a means of tackling its declining economic strength?

Fidel Castro: The United States, engaged as it is in military adventures of various kinds and in the arms race, has lost much of its ability to compete in many branches of the economy, where it used to have a leading position. The cars that used to come from the United States now come from Japan. Nowadays, a large part of the cars that are used in the United States itself, either come from Japan or are made in the United States by Japanese companies. And the same is true with electronics, household appliances, equipment for the machine industry, the petrochemical industry, the chemical industry and many other fields. The United States wants to corner the market of 400 million Latin Americans as an investment market for high-yield capital, as a market for its products and as a source of cheap raw materials and cheap labor. What else is that capital looking for here in Latin America?

Logically, it won't be easy for it, either. It's also coming up against some kind of domestic resistance, because workers are worried about the consequences. The unions and some industries are becoming worried, especially branches that employ many workers and aren't vanguard industries. But the politicians, big industry and the big monopolies aren't going to oppose having the United States seize the Latin American market and make it a part of its economy. If that happens and the United States doesn't meet any resistance, we Latin Americans will have — historically speaking — ceased to exist and there's no telling what we will be — perhaps a possession of the United States. Those are the things I'm worried about and what I fear.

Now, when Bush talked about the Initiative, everybody applauded, but I'm not sure why. I don't think anybody has really studied its consequences. It was superficial applause, but universal. Then they began to think — I imagine that a lot of people are now thinking — but the analysis hasn't been based on a serious, in-depth study of the consequences it will have.

Beatriz Pagés: Even so, Latin America — especially Mexico — has pinned all its hopes to the development of a free trade agreement and to the Initiative for the Americas.
Fidel Castro: We need to keep in mind that the Initiative doesn't offer any solution for the problem of the region's foreign debt. Between 1982 and 1990, Latin America transferred $220 billion to its creditors, but it still owes $434 billion. The reduction of around $7 billion of its official debt to the U.S. government is insignificant — not even 2 percent of the accumulated debt — and the problem remains the same. It is absolutely necessary to solve it in order to even think about renewing Latin America's economic growth.

The fund of $300 million a year that the Initiative proposes for stimulating capital investments in the region — of which the United States would contribute only $100 million — is simply ridiculous. It falls far short of meeting the needs that Latin America has accumulated in the course of a decade of profound economic and social crisis. This is a region in which no less than

40 percent of the population lives in poverty, a region that sends $300 million abroad every three days in interest payments on its foreign debt.

Another basic aspect is the economic integration of Latin America and the Caribbean. What will become of it when faced with this Initiative? The U.S. proposal tries to tie the countries to the U.S. market by means of bilateral agreements, but what space will remain for the already minimal trade among the Latin American countries, which accounts for only 14 percent of the region's total exchanges?

Under this proposal, the U.S. economy will swallow up the Latin American economies. This will lead to the destruction of the little regional integration that has been achieved and will keep that process, which is of vital importance for Latin America and the Caribbean, from progressing in the future.

Beatriz Pagés: Every time the U.S. trade authorities sit down to negotiate with their Latin American counterparts concerning the agreement or the Initiative, everybody pledges reciprocity or mutual exchange. Is such equality possible between two economies that are so different, not only in composition but also in strength?

Fidel Castro: The topic of mutual exchange is well worth considering. How can they speak of mutual exchange between parties as unequal as the United States and Latin America? Between parties with such great differences in terms of economic development, reciprocity would simply be the consolidation of unequal terms of trade, one of the most brutal forms of pillaging in the present era.

It is deplorable that, so far, Latin America's response to the Initiative hasn't even stated firmly that reciprocity should be partial or relative. The difference in levels of development that keeps Latin America from making trade concessions as speedily as the United States should also be acknowledged. This seems to me to be an elementary statement for the defense of Latin America, because of the difference in the levels of economic development. Everybody knows that the current U.S. Foreign Trade Act has buttressed protectionism, shutting out Latin

American products, while at the same time, the United States is demanding that the countries of the region eliminate all of their own protective mechanisms.

I'm speaking of the picture I have of the intentions of the United States and what may be behind the Initiative. There is no more selfish country on the face of the Earth than the United States. There is no country that is less generous in its economic policy, no country that is more voracious than the United States. What can we expect from that empire? It is already talking about a new era, about a Pax Americana and a new U.S. world order that will last for 1,000 years. We should find out what our role will be as Latin Americans and what our identity will be as Latin Americans in that new order of which the United States is dreaming.

These things must still be answered. I think that we should all meditate and study the situation in depth to get a clear idea of what lies ahead.

Beatriz Pagés: Going back to your reflections, what role should we Latin Americans play in the proposed trade bloc integrating Latin America with the United States?

Fidel Castro: The first thing we should do is to study it seriously and in depth. We have to come up with some clear ideas about all this, because everything is very diffuse, very generic, even very confusing. Analyzing this new international situation that has been created — all these new communities that have been formed or strengthened in the new economic balance of forces in the world — we must decide what really is best for our countries' economies. We can't join in the applause for a certain initiative when nobody knows exactly what it means. The Mexicans, at least, have been discussing it for some time, trying to find out exactly what it all means. But the other Latin American countries have applauded it when they really don't know what it's all about.

We ask what price we will have to pay if we do away with tariff barriers — will the price be the ruination of all our industries?

Thinking about the problem as Latin Americans, what specifically would be left to the Latin Americans in that world, that order, that integration? What would be left to them and what would it mean to them if they are separated from Japan, Europe and the rest of the world? What specifically would that U.S. economic initiative mean for all of the Americas? That hasn't been studied.

Beatriz Pagés: In view of Latin America's enormous economic and social needs, this integration seems inevitable.

Fidel Castro: What seems inevitable is that the Latin American countries will do what the United States wants. It is laying down the guidelines and dictating the terms of what must be done. There should at least be a united front of all Latin America to analyze the problem, with the economists and scientists showing us the consequences — but in a practical, objective way; it isn't a matter of fighting an idea with slogans.

Beatriz Pagés: Cuba has become a kind of bumper for the Latin American car, because it is the first to be hit by U.S. power, high-handedness and intolerance. Do you think the nations of the region realize that, if the Cuban regime should fall as a result of U.S. intervention, it would also endanger the sovereignty of the rest of Latin America?

Fidel Castro: Many Latin Americans fear that, but whether or not they say so publicly is another matter. Many sectors, public figures and governments in Latin America are aware that we constitute the front line, and that if this front line — that cannot be bribed or defeated — should fall, the independence of the rest of Latin America would be dealt a terrible blow. The modest independence gained would lose what is now its best shield. Who could resist if the United States should get its way and crush this bulwark that has stood firm against it in so many and such difficult situations? The bells would toll not only for Cuba but for all of Latin America.

Beatriz Pagés: What will be the future of Panama following the U.S. invasion of that country and Guillermo Endara's rise to power?

Fidel Castro: Endara didn't rise to power — the U.S. authorities put him there.

I think that Panama's future won't be very different from that of the other Latin American countries, because the United States may try to turn all of us into Panamas. I think that Panama will go where Latin America goes; the Panamanian people will go where the other Latin American peoples go.

The immediate future is already known: the United States intends to remain there indefinitely as the owner or controller of the Canal and its military bases. This was the real purpose of the invasion of Panama — simply, to throw out the Torrijos-Carter Agreements and to indefinitely maintain its military bases there. I don't know what benefit we Latin Americans can derive from that. In the immediate future, the most probable thing is that the United States will manage to impose the articles that will allow it to maintain its bases.

It is still militarily occupying that country. Still! Meanwhile, it has waged a war 15,000 kilometers away, in the Arab-Persian Gulf, using the pretext of Iraq's occupation of Kuwait.

Those are the characteristics of the new order that the United States wants to impose on the world. Either the Panamanians will be saved along with the others, or they'll go down with them.

Beatriz Pagés: How do you explain Violeta Chamorro's rise to power in Nicaragua? Is it a popular rejection of Marxism-Leninism?

Fidel Castro: I don't think it has anything to do with Marxism-Leninism, because the Nicaraguans didn't try to apply Marxist-Leninist principles. The only way they applied any of those principles was in not trying to build socialism in Nicaragua. It would not have been advisable to apply Marxism-Leninism there, where not even the minimal conditions existed for building socialism. The Sandinistas never proclaimed socialism in Nicaragua. Instead, they applied a model that included both public and private ownership, as has been done in nearly all of the Latin American countries. Right from the start, they established a multi-party system.

They did confiscate Somoza's property and because Somoza

had owned so much the government's share was considerable. They carried out a thoroughgoing agrarian reform and many other measures of a social nature to benefit the people, but the Mexican Revolution adopted measures just as radical as the Sandinistas in terms of agrarian reform. Therefore, it can't be interpreted as a rejection of socialism, because nobody tried to build socialism there.

The U.S. authorities, who didn't want to forgive the Sandinista Revolution for being independent and progressive, subjected it to a dirty and ruthless war that ruined the economy, took tens of thousands of lives and forced the country to make enormous sacrifices. It was this that determined the election results: the United States, which was responsible for the war, promised peace if the Sandinistas were voted out of office; the United States, which was imposing the economic blockade, promised to lift it and economically assist Nicaragua if the Sandinistas were voted out; it promised the Nicaraguans everything. Essentially, it promised that a change of government offered the solution to the economic problems and bring about peace in the country. This had an undeniable effect that was decisive in the election.

I'm not going to say that was the only factor, because an election is an election, and the result also depends on who has more ability in running their campaign and addressing the issues, what image they convey, and their resources. In a contest of that kind, both objective and subjective factors play a role. It's logical that, if the revolutionaries' party is involved in a contest of that kind, it will have plenty of talent, wisdom and experience for winning the battle in that political arena. The leaders, the individuals, may have made mistakes, or there may have been mistakes in the message that was conveyed — all that has an influence, it is only logical. But the main factor in the defeat of the Sandinistas was the economic and political weakening caused by the dirty war imposed by the United States and its promise that there would be peace and economic solutions if the Sandinistas were voted out of office.

So far, they have achieved a relative peace. But that peace is largely due to the care and wisdom with which the Sandinistas have acted. There is peace — not because of anything the United

States has done, but mainly because of the contribution the Sandinistas have made since the election by respecting and obeying the results of the election, an election that was held in the midst of political and economic conditions that were very difficult for them. Nobody can deny that they have done everything possible to achieve peace. As for the economic situation, imperialism's cooperation and "aid" to Nicaragua, as in Panama, have been miserly, ridiculous and laughable.

Beatriz Pagés: What is your opinion of Violeta Chamorro?
Fidel Castro: I should say in her favor that, as I see it, Violeta Chamorro has acted with moderation. She hasn't made any extreme changes, in the sense of undoing what had been carried out by the Sandinistas. I think that the careful, moderate way in which she has acted, faced with the rightist extremist groups that supported her, has also facilitated the search for peace.

The relations between our two countries have been maintained and have been normal, respectful. Her triumph hasn't meant a breaking of relations between our countries. As far as possible, the exchanges and cooperation between Nicaragua and Cuba have been maintained. It is only fair to recognize her contribution in this regard, too.

Beatriz Pagés: Apart from exceptional cases, the guerrillas are no longer a presence in most Latin American countries. Do you think that the conditions which gave rise to those revolutions, or to the existence of guerrillas, in Latin America no longer exist? Could we say that the era of revolution has already passed?
Fidel Castro: No, nobody can say that the era of revolution has passed. I told you that at the beginning. This is because the objective conditions for revolution haven't passed. Far from it: they are ever more acute.

The subjective factors have changed, however. This is a moment of great political confusion. There is great confusion even in the left because of all the problems that have arisen in Eastern Europe and in the international revolutionary movement. Some people are even sorry they were ever leftists; sorry they were communists or socialists. We are witness to all of this, including expressions of cowardice and opportunism. Above all, there is perplexity among the forces of the left, including the revolutionary forces, which is a logical consequence of what has happened and also, I think, corresponds to a transitory period. This, too, will pass.

Changes have taken place in the politics of Latin America; objective conditions have changed. A democratic opening has been created in many of the countries that had been subjugated to harsh military dictatorships. Logically, this has meant a change in the objective conditions, since possibilities for peaceful, political struggle now exist in those countries. This also influences the tactics that revolutionaries and other leftists should use.

Even though the government in our country was very corrupt, it never occurred to us to begin a guerrilla struggle in a constitutional period, when means of political struggle were available. We turned to guerrilla struggle only after Batista's coup of March 10, 1952. As a revolutionary, I always believed from then on that we would have to seize power through a revolution with the people's support and that society could not be changed without a revolution, without a revolutionary power. Every revolution requires the right political, economic, social and historical circumstances — among other things, an acute, unsolvable crisis.

Ever since the beginning of the Revolution, I have said that, wherever the conditions for political struggle existed, political struggle rather than armed struggle should prevail. In the First and Second Declarations of Havana — you can look this up, if you like — we said that armed struggle should take place only where all other avenues were closed, as a last resort, as a response to repression that made political struggle impossible. Those circumstances — along with poverty, misery and the general crisis of society — were ideal objective conditions for revolutionary struggle.

Kennedy understood those objective conditions well: after the [1961] Bay of Pigs invasion of Cuba and its subsequent failure, fearing that the Cuban Revolution might be repeated in other Latin American countries, he launched the project of the Alliance for Progress and promised billions of dollars and actually did provide some of the money. He asked for reforms, proclaimed reforms, and the United States, that had never before accepted the term "agrarian reform" because it considered it a communist concept, now called for an agrarian reform, fiscal reforms and social programs. That is, faced with the Cuban Revolution, Kennedy was forced to launch an initiative and to proclaim the need for reforms in Latin America, because he understood that the objective factors could give rise to revolution in this hemisphere. At that time, Latin America had only half as many inhabitants as now and less than half as many unemployed, people in hunger and misery. Moreover, it didn't owe a cent. Now, 30 years later, Latin America has two or three times as many problems — that is, its objective social conditions have worsened. But the objective political conditions have seen some changes for the better in recent years, such as the transition from repressive governments, military dictatorships, and tyrannies, to a democratic opening which, even though it doesn't solve any economic or social problems — which are growing ever more acute — does provide means for political struggle.

When we were discussing the problems of the foreign debt and other economic problems in 1985, I said that socialism wasn't on the agenda for Latin America. But what was on the agenda were independence and the creation of the conditions for Latin America's development — without which it wouldn't even be possible to think about a subsequent advance toward socialism.

In those special conditions, I wasn't calling for domestic struggle. To the contrary, I was calling for unity inside each country and unity among the countries so we could confront the tragedy of the debt, wage a vital battle in the great economic sphere, achieve independence and ensure our peoples' survival. I said that, if the conditions didn't exist for development, there couldn't be any development — neither capitalist nor socialist. The day when the era of change and of socialism come, the countries will need the resources and capacities for development, independence and a world economic order; without them, socialism cannot be built in Latin America.

That's what I said in 1985. Some people didn't like it, but I was proposing those tactics and that strategy in 1985. I said that the workers, farmers, students, professionals, middle strata, national businessmen and other social forces should unite, and the different countries should join forces to wage that battle.

The speeches and statements are all there; it isn't anything new. I don't think socialism is on the agenda for Latin America now, and wherever the possibilities for political struggle exist, political means should be used.

In the present subjective conditions of the revolutionary movement in Latin America, I don't think the conditions are favorable for armed struggle. Therefore, I have concentrated my efforts, my comments, in this direction: that of struggling to find a solution for our countries' economic problems and struggling to achieve unity among the countries of Latin America.

I advocate a common front for meeting the great challenge that lies ahead. I don't advocate armed struggle. It was correct in a certain stage of Latin America's political process, in different situations. However, the conditions aren't exactly alike in all countries. There are some exceptional cases, as you said in your question, in which the people have alternatives to using armed struggle, even if only to open up political means of struggle.

Beatriz Pagés: How would you explain the case of Fujimori in Peru?

Fidel Castro: The explanation of the Fujimori case lies in the discredit into which the traditional parties and traditional politics have fallen, with the people desperate, with no hope of seeing their political problems solved.

The fact that someone can rise up overnight and win the support and votes of most of the population against all forecasts is a consequence of the crisis of politicians and parties.

Beatriz Pagés: Did you expect Vargas Llosa to have a landslide victory?

Fidel Castro: It seemed inevitable that he would win and the first one to think so was Vargas Llosa himself. According to all of the traditional norms and old politics, he should have won a landslide victory. Those calculations didn't include any provision for a man such as Fujimori. The vote was also a rejection of the conservative programs and the policy that Vargas Llosa was promoting.

I think that, in addition to the traditional parties and politicians being discredited, the people have shown wisdom in rejecting the brutal formulas of neoliberalism. This was also a contributing factor in the Fujimori case. The people are learning.

Beatriz Pagés: Who knows if he offers any real hope?

Fidel Castro: During a recent meeting with bankers, I told one of them, "Look, the governments aren't always to blame for everything; the governments can't solve problems." He had been arguing that the problems were caused by inflation and I don't know what else, by government policies.

I told him, "The situation in our underdeveloped countries is so bad — with such enormous accumulated social needs, the debt, economic dependence, chaos, corruption and such a terrible international economic order — that, even if you got the best person, the wisest and most intelligent of all the saints, to come down from Heaven and put them in office in those conditions, they would fail. The situation is so bad that nobody can remedy it." I told him that, because he was trying to blame all of those problems on government policy. I said, "Then all governments, without exception, are bad, because all of them, without exception, have failed; none has managed to solve the problems." I can't accept his thesis. I would say that the conditions that exist in those countries are so bad that, even if you brought in the most perfect, wisest and most intelligent person — maybe Solomon, Lycurgus or another of those very wise rulers in history — and put them there, they would be politically ruined within six months, a year or two years. No matter how much they wanted to solve the problems, they wouldn't be able to do so. They would be doomed to fail. This isn't a matter of individuals; it is a question of national and international systems.

CHAPTER 7

A meeting of two cultures?

Beatriz Pagés: What is Cuba's position on the 500th Anniversary of the Discovery of the Americas celebrations? Should it be called the discovery of the Americas or should it be called a meeting of two cultures?

Fidel Castro: That is a very sensitive and polemical topic. I have already expressed my opinion on this.

I remember that in 1985, six years ago, when we were discussing the debt, I expressed some opinions that led some in Spain to react to this. My view is that there should be a critical 500th anniversary celebration, not just an apology for the 500th anniversary.

There are many merits in the history of navigation and the voyages of Columbus. Moreover, he was a very outstanding personality with great merits as a scientist, a courageous person, a discoverer in the sense that a scientist who is testing theories about nature is a discoverer. Among other things, he proved that the Earth was round. That theory had been voiced ever since the time of Ptolemy, but he had the courage to confront superstition and all the theories in vogue that said the Earth was flat. He believed in the theory that the Earth was round, and his own history, his perseverance, his tenacity and his voyages are worthy of admiration. Those are really positive things.

However, the discovery brought with it some very terrible phenomena for our peoples — such as the conquest. We were, in fact, conquered. Nobody knows what laws were invoked to justify conquering us, unless it was the law of the jungle. Moreover, the conquerors colonized and enslaved us, forcing the original inhabitants of this hemisphere to mine gold and silver, with the result that the original inhabitants were nearly exterminated. Some groups of them, as in Cuba, practically disappeared.

In Santo Domingo, terrible wars were waged against the Indians. I think it was Washington Irving, one of Columbus's biographers, who described them. I read it some years ago: how many organized groups of Indians there were in Santo Domingo and how courageously they fought — they were great fighters — but, even so, they were exterminated.

Everybody knows what happened in the rest of Latin America. Of the 6 or 7 million Indians in Mexico, to cite just one example, only a third were left. That is, the discovery also brought about the semi-enslavement or enslavement of the Indians and their virtual extermination in many places.

The third phenomenon is that the discovery led to modern slavery and the bringing to this hemisphere of tens of millions of Africans who were enslaved.

The conquest, colonization, extermination and slavery were all linked to the discovery.

I wonder if, in these modern times, we can make an historical abstraction of those realities that accompanied the discovery, if we can forget about the value of freedom and the rights of humans to such an extent that we forget all of the negative factors that followed the discovery. That's why I said that a critical historical analysis should be made, because there are those who want to discover us again and conquer us again now, and it seems a little absurd to me that, 500 years from now, people may be eulogizing this new discovery, too.

Since these are historical events, we should analyze them with historical objectivity, not hatred. This isn't inspired by any feeling of hatred toward any country — least of all, Spain — or toward Europe. Really, the criticism I would make is inspired by the defense of certain values that cannot be renounced. The Spanish had a history of 700 years of war and they flooded this hemisphere with warriors. Well, that doesn't make me sad; it might almost be said that I'm glad they brought us the genes of courageous, combative people, people who fought for their independence, and they were mixed with the genes of our Indians, who were also very courageous. I have already told you the history of Santo Domingo and of the other original inhabitants of this part of the world. I think it was a good mixture: Spanish, Indian, and African. We are a product of that history. Therefore, far from being motivated by any anti-Spanish feeling, my position was based on a respect for certain historical and moral values.

Now, more than ever, we should fight against any conquering, colonizing, pillaging and exploiting spirit, because the peoples of the world — mainly the billions of people who live in the Third World — are interested in having the principles of national independence and peoples' rights respected and in fighting against everything that violates those principles.

Some comrades and visitors have spoken of a "meeting of two cultures." That is the elegant — pious, if you like — way of referring to those historical events. In fact, one culture came and was imposed on another. It wasn't a meeting; it was the crushing of one culture and some peoples by others whose military technology was more developed. But now people are calling it a "meeting of two cultures."

That's the position I have upheld on all this. I also think that we should acknowledge the positive aspects of everything that has happened. We received some good things from Europe — not only wrongs and diseases. To cite just one example, we got our language from the Spanish, and, thanks to it, we can all communicate; if we still spoke the languages of our predecessors, we wouldn't understand one another very well in Latin America. The Spanish also contributed certain norms of organization and juridical principles, plus their rich culture — which, even though it prevailed, still mixed to some extent with the one that was here, that made many contributions to our present culture, just as the Africans also made important contributions to it. Many literary and cultural values came from the Old World, and we should be glad about this.

Also, it must be said to the credit of the Spanish that, unlike the Anglo-Saxons, they mixed with the Indians and Africans. In North America, the Anglo-Saxons wiped out almost all of the Indians; they wanted to exterminate them as a matter of principle, considering them unworthy of mixing with the whites and not deserving the right of existence. The Spanish didn't have those prejudices; they mixed with both the Indians and the Africans. The Spanish didn't exterminate the Indians in order to wipe them out. Rather, they exterminated them in the course of exploiting and extracting wealth from them; that's another concept.

Lastly, I should say frankly that I am glad we were colonized by the Spanish rather than the Anglo-Saxons. The Spanish had another character, which led to what was created: a truly new world, the product of all that mixing.

That is, I don't have a sectarian position or any wish to harass, bother or wound anybody with these ideas. That is the point of view I have upheld on this polemical matter. We have cooperated with the activities and we will keep on cooperating. When there is a fair in Seville, we will send representatives to Seville; when there are Olympic Games in Barcelona, we will send representatives to Barcelona; when Spanish ships came, repeating Columbus's voyage, we welcomed them here — I have met more than once right here, in this same building, with young people who came on those ships. That is, we have cooperated fully with the activities, but we have also maintained our position — without making an issue of it, because we haven't wanted to cause any conflict.

I have been in contact with many representatives of indigenous groups in Latin America. I have talked with them and know what they think. They have a very critical, extremely critical, position on everything related to the 500th anniversary. They have their demands, their claims, and they speak very eloquently and strongly when defending their point of view. Really, it's very moving to speak with those descendants of the indigenous communities who remain in many parts of Latin America. I think that their point of view should be heard and made known.

If all this is kept in mind, we could have a more balanced celebration that would be fairer, historically speaking. As I told you, it should be a critical celebration, looking for the positive aspects and recognizing the negative ones.

Moreover, not all countries have the same position, because not all had the same history. Mexico has one position; so do

Ecuador and Peru. Many more Indians survived in some countries than in others. There are some Latin American countries in which the Indians practically disappeared, though they left some traces. You find this in Argentina, which is very European; the Indians left their mark there, as you can see in some of their features. But 80 or 90 percent of the people in some countries are of European descent. They were landing points for millions of European émigrés not long ago, and, logically, they don't have the indigenous traditions that Peru, Mexico, Ecuador, Bolivia, Guatemala and some other countries have. There are many countries that have a strong indigenous tradition and a strong indigenous presence in the composition of their populations; in others, you see it less. This explains the different approaches.

I also found two attitudes. I found when I was in Mexico that the Mexicans didn't want to hear Cortes's name mentioned, and some of the terms you Mexicans use when you want to describe somebody — terms dating from the time of the conquest — are well known. In Peru, however, the people preserve Pizarro's body with respect. That is, their conduct was different, and the subsequent processes have also been different.

The indigenous peoples played an important role in Mexico's independence and the Mexican Revolution, but in parts of South America they were swayed by a realist influence during the struggle for independence. In some places in Latin America, there was a great realist influence in the indigenous communities; in some countries in the south, the fighters from Venezuela and Colombia were even viewed with distrust.

There has been a little of everything, hasn't there? San Martín wanted to set up a monarchy that would consist of Argentina, Chile and Peru (including Upper Peru), because he didn't think the conditions existed for another form of government. In the Viceroyalty of Peru, however, there was a very strong oligarchy that took a rather ambiguous stance during the war of independence.

San Martín came to believe that that Peruvian oligarchy — which unquestionably was the strongest and most consolidated in South America — was called upon to play an important role in the constitution of a monarchy, and historians say he even talked about this with a French prince.

This shows you the different historical processes in the various countries — and, therefore, the different ways in which they are more or less sensitive to the 500th anniversary and how they react to it.

Beatriz Pagés: Just one more question about this topic: In view of this heightened sensitivity, shouldn't the governments of the various Latin American countries try to overcome this resentment?

Fidel Castro: I don't have any objections to ending resentment, but that can only be done on the basis of justice, truth, acknowledgement of what historical events were really like and a critical spirit — that would be of greater assistance. Ignorance of the facts of history can produce more resentment.

Many of those indigenous communities are experiencing terrible poverty now.

When the Pope visited Ecuador and Bolivia, he met with hundreds of thousands of Indians. In many places, they experience terrible poverty, educational backwardness, no schools, no hospitals, no jobs and no land. It's a great tragedy. Now, 500 years after the discovery, many of those indigenous communities are still suffering from the tragedy brought by the discovery. Who is going to convince them not to be resentful? How could anybody do that?

There is a lack of social justice in all our countries. As long as social justice doesn't prevail, I seriously doubt that anybody is going to think about the plight of those Indians or indigenous communities and their suffering.

I would agree to burying resentment. It's necessary, because we aren't going to keep on harboring resentments dating from the time of Adam and Eve and remain angry because Cain killed Abel. Just imagine: according to the Bible, there have been fratricidal struggles ever since humans first appeared. Logically, as a revolutionary and a socialist, I would like human beings to be brothers and sisters and for them to free themselves of all resentment — but it must be on the basis of justice and of historical acknowledgement of the truth.

CHAPTER 8
Cuba and the Pope

Beatriz Pagés: At one time there was a lot of publicity given to the possibility of visit of Pope John Paul II to Cuba. Why hasn't he come?

Fidel Castro: No agreement has yet been made. No definitive steps for such a visit have been taken. I would say that we have other priorities right now. Ever since the new problems arose on the international scene, we have been devoting all of our time and energies to matters that we consider vital in the special period. The subject of the visit hasn't even come up recently.

Beatriz Pagés: John Paul II is considered to be one of the most important architects of the current reforms that have been made in the socialist world. What is your opinion of the Pope and of his stand on socialism?

Fidel Castro: I can't see any basis for thinking that the Pope was the great strategist of what happened in Eastern Europe. The Pope may have influenced events in his own country and doubtless he does influence them because it is a Catholic country with a great Catholic tradition and strong ties between the people and the Catholic Church, for well-known historical reasons. He had very good relations with the authorities of that country; he visited several times and talked with them. Undoubtedly, he has had more influence there than in the other Eastern European socialist countries. The Church has had an historical influence, but I don't think that's reason to call the Pope the strategist for political change, even in Poland. There would be even less reason for saying he was responsible for the political changes in Romania, Hungary, Czechoslovakia and the German Democratic Republic. I think that other factors were responsible for those changes.

Moreover, that thesis would be tantamount to assuming that the Pope engaged in flagrant intervention in the internal political affairs of those countries. I think we would be making an unfounded charge against him if we were to draw that conclusion; I don't consider it objective.

I have to view the Pope in his triple role: first, as the head of a church — not only the spiritual but also the real head of that church. He has been one of the most active heads that church has had in recent times, one who has moved around the most and acquired the greatest ascendency and authority, both inside and outside that church. He has, really, been a very active Pope. In that regard, I could also say that he has been an able Pope as head of the Catholic Church — that is my opinion.

The second aspect is his role as head of the Vatican, a government with which we have normal, respectful relations.

But as the carrier of certain ideas and politics that are unquestionably opposed to socialism, the Pope espouses ideas that I don't share. I don't share his opposition to socialism; I can't share those ideas at all. From that ideological point of view, there are differences between my views and those of the Pope. Even so, I have appreciated the occasions when the Pope has spoken out criticizing aspects of capitalism, such as when he criticized poverty on his trips through Latin America. On occasion, he has met with hundreds of thousands of Indians and they have told him they don't have jobs, food or land. In reply he has given them words of encouragement. Likewise, when he visited slums, the slum-dwellers told him they had no work and their children were dying of sickness and hunger. He expressed his solidarity with those sectors. When he has said that the farmers need land, the workers need jobs, and the children need health care, food and schools, I have agreed with him.

Some people point out that, while making some criticisms of capitalism, he has practically ruled out socialism. I don't share the view that the era of socialism has passed. I think that it is very far from having passed, for the reasons I have given in this interview.

Beatriz Pagés: Couldn't the Pope become an important intermediary at some point for smoothing over the differences between Cuba and the United States?

Fidel Castro: He's never been asked to serve as an intermediary and I don't have the faintest idea whether or not the United States would be interested in that. A task of that kind would require the consent of both parties. Really, I don't think that the relations between Cuba and the United States could be helped by the actions of an intermediary, no matter how brilliant they might be. Unless God Himself would come down to Earth and change the world, change the mentality of imperialism, and challenge the very existence of imperialism. We could then have a neighbor that would coexist with us and respect our country's sovereignty.

I think it would take a very great miracle and the one who works miracles is in Heaven, not on Earth, and we don't have many means of communication with Heaven. Therefore, I seriously doubt that any intermediary could do what is needed to improve the relations between Cuba and the United States. This is apart from the goodwill of the Pope, who has succeeded in settling some international conflicts.

Many people want the relations between Cuba and the United States to improve. Some politicians and others are doing whatever they can to improve our relations. We appreciate their efforts and are grateful for them. But we are also very aware that, at this time of exaggerated triumphalism in the United States, when they express such extreme chauvinism, there is very little chance that U.S. relations with Cuba will improve. At this time, when the U.S. authorities believe that the Revolution is about to burst and that the Revolution won't be able to stand firm because of what has happened in Eastern Europe, it is very unlikely that the United States will be interested in improving its relations with Cuba.

Beatriz Pagés: Do you believe in miracles?

Fidel Castro: Certainly, I believe in the miracles of what work, science and humanity can achieve. I believe in the miracles of what humans can do with their love, intelligence, determination, heroism and goodness. I believe in those miracles. As for others, I haven't seen any convincing proof of them.

CHAPTER 9

Dreams and ambitions

Beatriz Pagés: What dreams and ambitions do you have at this point in your life?

Fidel Castro: I imagine that, when you say "at this point," you mean now that I am over 60 — or, rather, after a long participation in the revolutionary struggle.

Very briefly, I would say that they are the same dreams and aspirations I had when I first considered myself a revolutionary, a long time ago. I continue to dream the same dreams, to think exactly the same way and to want the same things.

Beatriz Pagés: What told you inside that you were a revolutionary?

Fidel Castro: I think that everybody has something of the revolutionary: a lack of conformity and a rebelliousness. There are circumstances that turn people into revolutionaries: the era, the historical conditions, the social situation in which they live, and the profound experiences in their lives. I wasn't born a revolutionary, but I was born rebellious. I had a chance to express my rebelliousness because personal experiences forced me to rebel when I was still very young — I've spoken about this on other occasions and I'm not going to repeat it here — when I was in the first grade and then in the fifth grade. Several times in my life I have had to rebel against things that didn't seem fair to me. And, at some point, I became aware of that.

There's a book called *La forja de un rebelde* (The Making of a Rebel) — I started reading it, but I haven't finished. It occurs to

95

me that a rebel is made partly by life, by their own experiences.

To be a rebel, you also need a certain temperament. I think a person's character or temperament has an influence: some people are more active than others; some are more affected by things than others. You're born with your character, but this isn't the only thing that determines whether or not you become a rebel. You can be born with a rebellious temperament yet be the most docile person in the world, depending on circumstances and your experiences.

I was born into a good economic environment; I didn't lack anything. Some of my experiences came from the fact that other people wanted to obtain economic benefits from my family and persuaded my parents to send us to the city to study. On some occasions, because of all those circumstances, I became aware of how interested in money some people were. All this formed the background for some of my experiences.

My parents were semi-illiterate farmers and lived in the countryside. They were farmers with land and trade, rich rather then poor farmers, but I also had a chance to see how others lived. That doesn't mean that I began to be a revolutionary at that moment, but during my vacations and at other times I saw how my friends and others lived. That experience as a child helped me a great deal many years later, when I began to think and analyze after I had graduated from senior high school and was beginning to study at university.

I was helped by everything I knew, starting with being one of the sons of a rich family, and everything I saw, such as how the other people there and in the vicinity lived — especially the workers on the large U.S.-owned sugarcane plantations, where the situation was much worse. The managers of those big companies were in New York, but my father was right there and people sought him out every day. He was a generous, kind man who tried to come up with solutions for the problems people asked him to solve — problems such as having five, six or more children but no work and nothing to eat. He always tried to find them some kind of work so the problem would be solved. In that sense, he was very generous, even though he thought as a land-owner and his ideology was that of a landowner.

I saw how the people lived. I have an indelible picture of what capitalism was like in the countryside, what things were like there up to the triumph of the Revolution. When I had a chance to come into contact with revolutionary and socialist ideas — although I started out by being a follower of Martí and still am one — I began with our country's history, its struggles, its wars of independence and its historical values. Those are the first things that motivate a national and patriotic spirit; the heroes in your country's history; and a sense of honor and of what is fair and unfair, what is good and bad. Starting from certain fundamental values, you begin making judgments, and if you add other historical values, all of those things create a political passion, a revolutionary passion. In me, that passion was multiplied when I came in contact with socialist ideas. That's how it was.

When I encountered Marx and Engels, Marxist literature opened my eyes to what society and history really were: I had never before found a coherent explanation of all that. Everything had seemed to be a result of chance, luck, chaos and anarchy. In Marxism, I found a coherent explanation of the history of humanity.

At first, as I have recounted on other occasions, I was a utopian socialist. Studying capitalist political economy, I began to think that it was all nonsense — and I still think it is — chaos and anarchy; and that it wasn't rational. That kind of society wasn't worthy of humanity. Then, when I discovered Marxist ideas, I ceased to be a utopian socialist and the coherence and clarity of Marx's ideas had an effect similar to that of putting a match to explosives.

I might have been a romantic revolutionary, a utopian, but I became a revolutionary when I acquired a political doctrine and a concept of society and became convinced that socialism was the fairest system. From then on, I was a revolutionary; I began to think in revolutionary terms.

The most important thing about all this may have been that I thought not only in terms of conceiving ideas, but also in terms of putting ideas into practice. Ever since I had revolutionary ideas, I always immediately thought about how to apply them — about not just how I, but how a group of people, a group of revolutionaries, should put those ideas into practice. At that point, I was alone. Later, I convinced a group of people, when I had already worked out most of the ideas.

I'm not going to go into this at any greater length, because it would take too long. I would have to explain what the political situation was like at that time and what we did. Here, I am simply answering your question of when I considered myself a revolutionary.

Beatriz Pagés: Yes, but one thing catches my attention: it is understandable that someone needy, a poor person, should become a revolutionary, but that isn't your case. Why did you turn your back on money, when many people think money gives you everything, including comfort?

Fidel Castro: If you analyze the history of nearly all revolutionary leaders, the same was true of them.

In general, people such as that poor farmer I knew there and the children of those poor agricultural workers didn't have an opportunity to go to school; they didn't have a chance to go to high school or university. I have thought about it. If I had been the son of one of those farmers or workers, I would never have become a revolutionary — or rather, I would never have come to play the part I did, the part I was called upon to play. I might have been a fighter in a guerrilla group that somebody organized; I might have been killed, or I might have survived. Most probably, I would have joined when all the poor farmers and agricultural workers joined the revolutionary struggle, but I couldn't have played the part of a leader.

I am known because of my role, but if I hadn't been able to study, if I hadn't been able to go to university, if I hadn't gotten in contact with those ideas, I wouldn't have been able to develop any revolutionary concepts and wouldn't have played an important role in the Revolution. I'm not going to say this applies to war, because sometimes leaders, brilliant warriors emerge — such as José Antonio Páez, a Venezuelan leader on the plains. He wasn't a Bolívar, a Sucre or like many of those other brilliant chiefs who had a high level of education; he was a practically illiterate farmer with great military talent. But leading a revolution, with all that it implies in terms of ideas, concepts and purposes, can only be carried out by people who have a certain level of education, of political culture. It isn't strange that many thinkers have come from the universities; as was the case with nearly all of the authors and theoreticians of socialism and nearly all of the most outstanding revolutionaries. Generally speaking, you have to come from at least the middle class to go to university. Poor people can't go there.

A person can become a revolutionary through ideas, independently of their class origin, and many people have done so. In our revolutionary process, many people of middle-class origin became revolutionaries. Generally speaking, the intellectual strata provide the theoretical contribution to the revolutionary process, even though they are workers' and farmers' revolutions.

In the Mexican Revolution, you have the case of Madero. Madero had an education. You had theoreticians and soldiers — both kinds of leader — in the Mexican Revolution. You had great soldiers who didn't have much cultural education, but they weren't the theoreticians of the Mexican Revolution. That is what explains the phenomenon, because people can become revolutionaries through ideas. Ideas have led people to do many things and make many sacrifices; there have been many selfless people in the world, who have given their lives for their ideas.

Rich landowners also took part in our wars of independence. It was mainly the landowners who initiated Cuba's wars of independence, slave owners with large landholdings. Carlos Manuel de Céspedes, a large landowner who also had a sugar mill, proclaimed independence on October 10, 1868, and freed his slaves. He was the first to do that. Those who conspired against Spain and began the War of Independence, risking their lives — many of them were killed, and nearly all of the survivors were ruined — those patriots were large landowners, from families of large landowners, the owners of land and slaves. They led the revolution in one period, until other leaders appeared who were closer to the people, fighters who made the struggle more democratic.

Cuba's history contains dozens and dozens of patricians, rich people, who began this country's most heroic war and one of the most heroic wars known in this hemisphere. They weren't socialists.

Rich people have often turned their backs on money for revolutionary reasons. Sometimes the revolution was of a bourgeois character. Some turned their backs on money to carry out the French Revolution or to carry out the revolutions in our own countries.

Bolívar was a very wealthy man, and his revolution wasn't socialist. Many other rich people joined Bolívar in the struggle for independence and gave their lives and all their wealth for that cause. Therefore, this isn't anything strange; the only difference is that, now, the revolution is for socialism.

My grandparents and great-grandparents weren't large landowners, but I was the son of a large landowner who lived in the countryside. He had been very poor, the son of poor farmers. My father was of Spanish origin. He worked hard, managed to make some money, bought land — land was cheap back then — and gradually came to have an important economic position, but he was the son of poor farmers. Thus, I didn't come from a family with a tradition as large landowners, with its landowner culture and class identification.

Merit isn't in individuals; it lies in the historical moment and the historical situation in which you're living. It doesn't matter how revolutionary someone's ideas may be; if they don't live in an historical period of revolutions, those ideas remain in their head and nothing comes of them. Therefore, no individual can claim the merit of starting a revolution, because a revolution is the fruit of many factors. You may have the privilege of being a revolutionary if you were born in an era in which that was possible. The individual contributes very little to all that.

If we had been born in the 17th century, what would we all have done? The thing is, we were born in the 20th century, in a certain historical situation, and that is what determines a revolutionary role. I wasn't the descendant of counts, marquesses or anything like that. I was the descendant of very poor farmers; my grandparents were very poor. My parents lived in the countryside, rubbing shoulders with ordinary people. That's what influenced me; I'm convinced of that.

Beatriz Pagés: A minute ago, you said you were a romantic, that you had always been a romantic. Are you the last romantic world leader left?

Fidel Castro: I didn't say "romantic" in that sense. I said that, if I hadn't had a revolutionary theory, I might have been a romantic revolutionary.

You use "romantic" in another sense. When I speak of romantics, I do so in the good sense, meaning dreamers who want things to be fair. That is, a revolutionary doesn't have to stop being a romantic in the good sense of the term. I used the word "romantic" to mean that I would have been dreaming of good things but wouldn't have had a revolutionary theory. It was in that sense I said "romantic." You can have a revolutionary theory and be romantic; you have to have at least a dash of romanticism to be revolutionary, to want to change things, to seek justice. Sometimes, however, the word "romantic" is used to refer to misguided people who have illusions and aren't realists.

Beatriz Pagés: Have you always been aware that you were a leader — and now a world leader?

Fidel Castro: I almost never think about it, but when, unfortunately, I do, I feel a tremendous burden of responsibility. I think about it in terms of the responsibility involved, not in terms of any satisfaction you may derive from considering yourself a leader or in terms of glory or honor. Naturally, we didn't wage our struggle for glory. I always remember something Martí wrote — one of the first things of his I read, and I have never forgotten it, because it contains a great truth. He said, "All the glory of the world fits in a kernel of corn." That was something truly admirable about Martí: he struggled for political goals, not glory.

In the time of those who fought for Latin American independence early in the last century, the fighters talked a great deal about glory. Bolívar was one; it was a constant theme with him. For them, glory was one of man's goals.

A modern revolutionary can't think about glory. We can't waste time feeling satisfied, thinking of honors and such things. Our satisfaction comes from the things we do, the successes we achieve. I tell you, you think quite a lot about the responsibilities you have and the problems that must be solved, and it's a great burden.

As for what you say about my being a "world leader," I have never thought about that. I swear, on my honor, that thought has never even entered my mind. This is a very small country, and the influence individuals have is measured by the influence their countries have on events.

You can put an idiot in as President of the United States — this has happened more than once — and he is a world leader; his country is a world leader. If you put an idiot in a position of power in a big country — and many big countries have had tremendous idiots — they are world leaders. But if you choose a person you consider ideal as a leader and put them in a position of authority in a small country, they aren't a world leader. A small country may come to have worldwide influence at a given time because it sets an example. It perhaps does things that are worthy of admiration; because it is heroic, or because it carries out great feats. A country can do that and have worldwide influence without being a world leader. Unquestionably, ideas have influence. I believe that ideas are the most important things.

World leaders are people who lead others. An international leader, a world-renowned leader, may even come to have some international influence. Influence can play a role — no doubt about that — but it is ideas, not individuals, that play the most powerful role in the world. We mustn't fail to recognize that.

Therefore, it wouldn't be correct to say that the leader of a small country such as Cuba could be a world leader.

The U.S. authorities made me famous. Many people admire Cuba, and the U.S. authorities are largely responsible for that because they focused attention on us. By turning me into their enemy, their adversary, they gave me more importance and made me more famous. They did this both with their slander and with their acts of hostility.

Yes, I know that I'm internationally known, I can see that in meetings, conferences and other things. But I have never thought in those terms or become conceited with the idea of being a world leader; it doesn't fit our possibilities.

Beatriz Pagés: What qualities should a Head of State have?

Fidel Castro: It depends on the country. If it is Switzerland, Luxembourg, Holland, Belgium or any other country that has a developed economy and a stable situation, they should probably be a specialist in economics, trading blocs and matters of integration — in short, a statistician-statesman rather than a politician, though it seems you also have to be a politician in order to be a statesman. They should have persuasive ability and communicate well — characteristics that suit those conditions.

What should a statesman in Haiti be like? The conditions that are required there, are unquestionably different from those required in Belgium and Holland and even in Uruguay. Haiti is a country with terrible poverty. In such a country, they should be someone in whom the people have very great trust. They should also be very charismatic, have the people's support, and be talented. They need to have the ability to do a great deal with very little, to assign correct priorities in the use of resources, to multiply the loaves and the fishes — in short, work miracles. I think that it requires much more ability to be a statesman in Haiti than to be one in a developed capitalist country, because the task is much more difficult in Haiti.

A Latin American statesman should, first of all, be a great patriot — and not just a patriot of their small or middle-sized country, but a patriot of Latin America as a whole. Secondly, they should be very honest and have a deep awareness of their responsibilities, great sensitivity for feeling the sufferings of others, a spirit of dignity and independence, and also, apart from knowledge, the ability to be advised: to choose those who can advise them and to assimilate their advice while not falling into the hands of technocrats. A statesman who depends only on their advisers and isn't very knowledgeable about the topics on which they receive advice, can fall prisoner to them. Thirdly, I think it is of the utmost importance in Latin America to now have an awareness of the need for integration and a very great sense of historical responsibility. If I were assigned the task of selecting Latin American statesmen, I would make sure that they met at least those requisites, but no two would be exactly the same, because each would have to fit the specific characteristics of the country in which they serve.

Politics has become very individualized. In answering your question, I have had to give personal opinions and speak of personal experiences. However, I think that the tasks of a revolution, a leadership and political work cannot be handled by individuals — and, as I already told you, our system is based not on individuals but on a group, a team.

Now, one person is nothing; they wouldn't be more than a military strongman. The era of military strongmen — a leader who gets people to do what he wants simply because all he has to do is ask — ended a long time ago. You can't conceive of a military strongman in socialism or in a modern revolution.

Here, we do things because we are thoroughly convinced of the need for them. We labor because we believe in an idea, a solution, a method.

That is, to analyze a process such as ours, you would have to reduce the role of individuals, no matter what their historical merits, and understand that their work forms part of that of a team, in which many people participate.

Beatriz Pagés: If you were faced with the unfortunate need to choose between death or political asylum in another country, which would you choose?

Fidel Castro: That certainly would be unfortunate, and it has never occurred to me to think about it. It wouldn't occur to me to think such a thing.

When we were in Mexico 35 years ago, in 1956, I made a promise. At a time when many people believed that the Revolution wouldn't come about and that we weren't going to return to fight, I told those people who wanted to sow scepticism, "In 1956, we will be free or martyrs" — a succinct summation. In 1956, we were free. We were already fighting in the Sierra Maestra mountains. We could also have been martyrs, but we returned to Cuba with our forces and began the struggle. We were in a section of free territory.

Since that time, for some 30 years, we have said "Homeland or death!" More recently we have added, "Socialism or death!" Our most sacred duty is to fight to the death defending our homeland

and the Revolution. There is no possible alternative. Don't forget that we have not only said "Homeland or death!," but also, "We will win." That is, we are confident in victory — not in personal victory, but in the victory of our cause, in the victory of the Revolution and the people.

I hope that I won't ever be faced with that unfortunate situation you mention, but I have no doubts at all about what I should and will do.

Beatriz Pagés: One last question. Because of your revolutionary activities, the previous regime imprisoned you, and as a lawyer you prepared your own defense, which ended with your famous sentence, "History will absolve me." Do you think that history has already absolved you, or must you still wait for that.

Fidel Castro: Well, I have to refer to two histories.

The first was that of our revolutionary struggle against Batista's dictatorship, which was victorious and ended with the complete social transformation of our country, with a true revolution. That is the meaning of what I said: you may condemn me now, but history will vindicate me, will prove me right.

Of course, history would have proved me right whether the Revolution had triumphed or not. I knew that the coming generations would vindicate me. But life itself, as well as the victorious Revolution, was further unequivocal proof that history had proved us correct.

Then came a second history, which is that of our struggle for more than 30 years against the mightiest imperialist power on earth. It is a history of Cuba's heroic resistance for all that time and the development of a socialist revolution on the doorstep of the United States. I am sure that that history, the second history, will also vindicate us. We are still engaged in that struggle, but the verdict of that history will be in our favor — I haven't the slightest doubt of that.

Beatriz Pagés: Thank you.

Related titles published by Ocean Press

Island in the Storm — The Cuban Communist Party's Fourth Congress (ISBN paper 1-875284-48-6)

The Cuban Revolution and the United States — A Chronological History (ISBN paper 1-875284-26-5)

An Encounter with Fidel
(ISBN paper 1-875284-21-4)

Changing the History of Africa
(ISBN paper 1-875284-00-1)

Fidel and Religion (ISBN paper 1-875284-05-2)

A New Society — Perspectives for Today's World by Che Guevara (ISBN paper 1-875284-06-0)

Cuban Women Confront the Future
(ISBN paper 1-875284-24-9)

The Right to Dignity — Fidel Castro and the Nonaligned Nations Movement
(ISBN paper 1-875284-02-8)